TEACHING SPELLING

a practical resource

TEACHING SPELLING

a practical resource

FAYE BOLTON & DIANE SNOWBALL

HEINEMANN
Portsmouth, NH

First published in the USA in 1993, reprinted 1994, 1996 (twice) by
Heinemann
a division of Reed Elsevier Inc.
361 Hanover Street Portsmouth, NH 03801-3912
Offices and agents throughout the world

First published in Australia in 1993 by
Thomas Nelson Australia
102 Dodds St.
South Melbourne, Vic 3205

ISBN 0-435-08802-5

Library of Congress Cataloguing-in Publication Data.

Bolton, Faye.
    Teaching spelling: a practical resource/Faye Bolton & Diane Snowball.
        p.   cm.
    Includes bibliographical references.
    ISBN 0-435-08802-5
    1. English language – Orthography and spelling – Study and teaching (Elementary)
I. Snowball, Diane. II. Title.
LB1574.B625 1993
372.6'32—dc20   93-8989
                                                                  CIP

Edited by Sandra Meredith
Designed and produced by Optima Consultants
Cover design by Optima Consultants
Printed in Melbourne by Impact Printing (Vic.) Pty Ltd

Contents

▼

▼

Introduction

The only authentic purpose for students to learn how to spell words in the conventional form is to assist others to read their writing. Students would even have difficulty in rereading their own writing if they did not develop some consistent spelling for the words they are using. Writing provides the purpose for spelling so students need to be helped with personal spelling needs for their own writing.

Although writing provides the purpose for learning how to spell, students will not necessarily become competent spellers just by writing frequently. Unless they continue to form hypotheses about how words are spelled, try these ideas, receive feedback and refine the hypotheses accordingly, the students' spelling may not develop into the conventional form.

Of course, the expression of ideas should be foremost in the writer's mind, but statements to students such as 'Spelling doesn't matter' can be misinterpreted as meaning 'Spelling doesn't ever matter' and 'There is no need to learn how to spell'. Learning how to spell in the conventional way *does* matter and there is a place in the daily classroom program for assisting students to do this.

This does not mean that the only context for teaching about spelling is when conferring with each individual student. It is appropriate to help an individual during an editing conference or at any other time they seek personal assistance, but it is also desirable to develop a class community of students who are interested in learning about the written language together.

In a previously published companion book, *Ideas for spelling* (Bolton and Snowball, Heinemann, 1993), detailed information is given about the nature of the English language and about the ways that students move from unconventional to conventional spelling. Ideas are provided for a classroom spelling program, with activities and assessment procedures. This book builds on those ideas, with Part 1 providing more specific information about management of the class program, details about goals and other means of assessment, and Part 2 providing resource lists of various types of words and activities related to those lists. The focus is on helping students to become competent spellers in authentic situations so that they realize the relevance of spelling for their own purposes.

The teaching of spelling, or helping students to learn about spelling, should be based on accurate knowledge about the English written language and knowledge about the strategies that competent spellers use.

The teacher can assist students to use such strategies and skills by helping them to notice the patterns and structure of the English language. This can be achieved through an enquiry approach so that students explore and discover information about the written language.

Class exploration is easily dealt with through reading any known material and searching for a particular feature of the language. This material may be the students' own writing, published books, magazines, poems, songs, or any environmental print, including class lists of words that have been developed in relation to topics the students may be writing about.

The exploration should be based on students' writing needs and should arise in the context of writing so that students are aware of the relevance of what they are learning. They should say or record what they have learned in their own wording so that it is personally meaningful and they should reflect on how this knowledge will help with their writing. Chapter 3 provides more information about how to plan class explorations and how to cater for individual needs.

Students will also be assisted with their personal spelling needs during writing conferences but it is helpful to be able to refer to class discussions about spelling, rather than only focusing on the correction of specific words.

This balance of class exploration and individual interest generates a positive attitude towards spelling and a continuing development of spelling ability.

Obviously the starting point is for students to perceive the need to write and to experiment with ways to use some form of written communication. Beginning writers need opportunities to write and materials to write with. Their spelling attempts should be valued and encouraged. Although there is no definite sequence of stages of development that every student will pass through there are common patterns that emerge with most students. Details about these may be found in *Ideas for spelling*. It is by observing these spelling attempts that the teacher is able to assess the students' spelling ability. Such observation guides the teacher in selecting the most pertinent aspects of written language to explore. In Chapter 4 further ideas about assessment are provided.

Naturally there will be many times when discussion about spelling will occur spontaneously and regardless of what the teacher may have planned these opportunities should not be ignored. The more learning about spelling is seen to be a process of enquiry and discovery about the written language, the more students are likely to notice about words when they are reading or writing and the more they are likely to raise issues for discussion. Although Chapters 5 to 11 provide resources for dealing with many aspects about written language, it is not necessary for teachers to feel that all elements of each chapter should be dealt with. The prime goal of every teacher should be to develop an interest in the nature of the written language so that students become independent learners who know what aspects are useful to learn about and how that learning can be of benefit to their writing.

The Basis for Teaching Spelling

1

Traditionally the teaching of spelling has involved the students learning a list of words by rote each week, usually selected by the teacher or decided by a commercial publisher. Or a spelling program may have been used that had little relevance to the students' writing and included activities that did not necessarily help students' spelling. Some of these activities may actually hinder students' spelling ability, such as those which purposely present words misspelled in a passage of text for students to proofread.

But learning how to spell is not only memorizing words and spelling activities should not be isolated from class and individual writing needs. A more sensible approach to the teaching of spelling is based on two main premises — learning about the written language and learning the strategies that competent spellers use.

▼ 1 Learning about the written language

The focus should be on learning about the relationships that exist between words in the written language rather than just learning individual words. The learning of selected words should only be a small part of the spelling program. Students should be helped to develop independence in spelling through acquiring knowledge about the written language that may be applied to any words they wish to write. This will provide them with much more power over writing.

The nature of the English written language is explained in detail in Chapter 2 of *Ideas for spelling* and Chapter 2 of this book provides further information.

▼ 2 Learning the strategies that competent spellers use

Competent spellers use many strategies to attempt and confirm the spelling of words when they are writing. (Chapter 2 provides more specific information about this.) Depending on the writer's language development and knowledge about the language the strategies may include the use of:

- knowledge about the various symbols used to represent each sound
- knowledge about common spelling patterns
- knowledge about the meaning relationships between words and how the meaning influences the spelling (e.g., words based on derivatives, words that are acronyms or eponyms, words formed by adding prefixes and suffixes to base words, compound words, words from other languages)
- knowledge about generalizations or rules that apply to many words.

Competent spellers also:

- attempt to spell unknown words
- are interested in and notice how words are spelled
- use memory aids to help remember part of a word (e.g., a **pie**ce of **pie**)
- refer to appropriate resources such as people, dictionaries, books, environmental print
- develop the habit of proofreading and editing their writing when it is necessary
- use a spell checker on a word processor, if available, to assist with proofreading

- know how to spell a body of words without needing to think about them
- remain up-to-date with current information about how words are spelled and are aware of alternative acceptable ways to spell some words.

The following table provides an overall comparison of how the teaching of spelling was dealt with in the past (and still is dealt with in some grades) and how it should be currently considered. This may help teachers to understand the importance of thinking about spelling in a way that really helps the learner. It may also help teachers and schools to make a transition from current practices to more useful practices.

The teaching of spelling before and now

Views about the English written language

Previously

English written language was thought to be a confusing language and highly inconsistent.

Currently

English written language is not confusing when viewed from the right perspective, that is from the meaning perspective rather than pronunciation.

Views about spelling

Previously

Spelling was viewed as a task of rote memorization, with learners told to learn individual words in isolation and not taught to think about the relationships that existed between the words. Students were not taught strategies for attempting to spell an unknown word.

Spelling was not viewed as being a developmental task in the same way as learning to speak.

Currently

Spelling is viewed as a problem-solving task that involves students in generating hypotheses about the way the English language works. Students learn about the relationships that exist between words and are taught strategies for attempting to spell an unknown word.

Spelling is viewed as a developmental task. Spelling competence is acquired over a period of time, depending upon the learner's experience with the English written language.

Spelling programs

Previously

The focus was on learning words.

All students learned exactly the same words, usually 10 or 20 words per week. Or students were grouped in spelling ability groups, with each group learning specified words.

Spelling was taught as a separate subject area and did not relate to other curriculum areas.

Currently

The focus is on learning about the written language and the relationships between words.

Individual students select words to learn for their personal writing needs. Thus the words selected and the number of words chosen vary from student to student.

The teaching of spelling is for the purpose of writing and involves learning about words from a range of curriculum areas.

Learning words

Previously

Students were expected to learn some words each week and not always shown how to do this.

Students were encouraged to develop memory aids for remembering words.

Some words were considered important to learn because they accounted for a large percentage of words written. The common word list was worked through and the words taught in isolation.

Correct spelling was highly valued in published pieces and was at times over-emphasized in pieces of writing not for publication.

Students were not allowed to write if they did not know how to spell correctly.

Currently

Students are expected to learn some words each week and are taught a systematic procedure for doing this, for example, the *Look, Say, Cover, Write, Check* procedure.

Students are encouraged to develop memory aids for remembering words.

Some words are considered important to learn because they account for a large percentage of words written. However, the words are taught in relation to other words with a common feature, be it spelling pattern, common sound or meaning relationship. Students are encouraged to generate such a list of words from their own reading and writing so that they realize the significance of learning how to spell them.

Correct spelling is highly valued in published pieces and is emphasized less in pieces of writing not for publication.

Students' approximations and inventing spellings are seen to be an important part of learning.

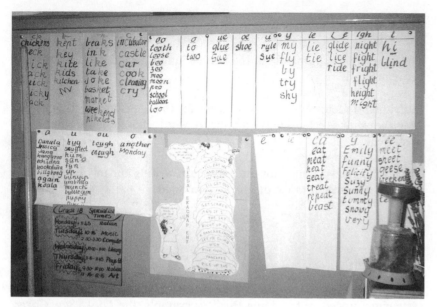

Class lists that focus on particular sounds.

A class list of compound words.

Word lists

Previously

Commercially published lists, unrelated to students' writing needs were provided and words were relegated to particular grade levels.

Words on the list were to be memorized by rote with very little thinking required.

Words were attributed levels of difficulty: two-letter words were supposed to be easier than three-letter words, which were supposed to be easier than four-letter words, and so on.

Some words were thought of as word demons or difficult words.

Currently

Classroom lists are written of words students want to learn for their personal writing needs, and words are not attributed to a particular year level.

Words on a list are not to be learned by rote but are listed to focus on a relationship (meaning, spelling pattern or common sound) that exists between words in the English written language.

It is now known that a word is not inherently difficult; a word is only difficult for a writer who has not seen it often or has not used it when writing. The number of letters in a word does not necessarily affect the student's ability to learn that word.

There is no need to give misleading and negative information.

Rules

Previously

Students were taught rules to which there were exceptions, and instructed to apply them.

Currently

Students are encouraged to generate hypotheses about the way the written language works and form generalizations. These are reviewed and refined as students' experiences with the language increases.

Using resources

Previously

Students were encouraged to refer to resources such as dictionaries and wordbooks often before they attempted to spell a word.

Currently

Students are encouraged to refer to resources such as dictionaries and wordbooks often to confirm their spelling attempts. They are also encouraged to find the most appropriate resource depending on the word.

Assessment

Previously

Dictation was used to test students' spelling competence, usually by the teacher marking the piece.

Currently

Dictation is not used to test students' spelling competence; other means of determining spelling competence are now used. It is not considered necessary to give dictation other than to find out how 'Safe Spellers' might attempt unknown words. Students would also be allowed to proofread the piece to find out what strategies they would use for attempting to correct the misspelled words.

Weekly spelling tests of words from published lists and dictation were the main type of assessment.

Weekly spelling tests of words from students' personal lists may be given for the benefit of the learner. Other data is also collected from students' writing, through observation, anecdotal records, and so on.

Whether a word was spelled correctly or not was the only consideration. The focus was on errors rather than on what the student could do.

Whether a word is spelled conventionally or not is not the only consideration. The strategies students use when attempting unknown words and their willingness to attempt unknown words are just some of the qualities considered and valued. Assessment begins with observing what the student can do and then focuses on something he/she could be helped with.

Proofreading

Previously

Teachers corrected students' writing or perhaps just put a mark through mistakes and sometimes students didn't even know why a word was wrongly spelled. This resulted in learning little other than a sense of failure.

Currently

Students learn to proofread and self-correct as much as possible. Other students or the teacher assist as an editor for published work. Not all writing needs to be proofread.

Letter names

Previously

Letter names were not always taught. Students were wrongly taught that the letter *a* was /a/ as in *cat*, the letter *o* was /o/ as in *cot*, and so on.

Currently

Letter names are taught. Students are taught that the letter *a* represents a variety of sounds, for example, /a/ as in *cat*, /o/ as in *salt*, /u/ as in *above*, and so on. The relationship that exists between a letter and the various sounds it represents are explored.

Good spellers

Previously

Students who spelled all words correctly were considered good spellers.

Currently

Students who spell all words correctly are not necessarily considered good spellers. It may be that they are not willing to attempt unknown words in their writing. Other qualities are highly valued.

Handwriting

Previously

Swift, legible handwriting was valued.

Currently

Swift, legible handwriting is valued.

Students' potential

Previously

People thought you were born a good or bad speller.

Currently

Everyone is capable of learning to spell well.

Achieving Spelling Competency

2

The attributes of a competent speller are listed below. It is logical that these should form the basis of a spelling program and be the framework for expected goals. Of course competent spellers also write frequently, particularly when they are learning about spelling. This provides both the purpose for learning and the opportunity to try out ideas about spelling and practise what they have learned. Also, the more that students read, the more likely they are to be competent at spelling. Reading provides the visual image for the recall of words, even though competent readers do not read word-by-word.

Attributes of competent spellers

Attitude

- Thinks he/she is a good speller.
- Attempts unknown words.
- Cares about spelling for publication.
- Takes an interest in words.

Habits

- Has a system for learning new words.
- Uses resources to confirm spelling attempts.
- Uses memory aids to help remember some words.

- Is willing to proofread.
- Writes legibly.

Word knowledge

- Has a developing body of known words.
- Knows the 100 most frequently used words.

Strategies

Phonetic
- Knows letter names.
- Knows that sounds can be represented by symbols.
- Knows that there are different spelling patterns for the same sound.
- Knows which spelling patterns represent each sound in the English language.
- Uses correct homophones.

Visual
- Knows that symbols are used to write words.
- Knows that letters are used to write words in the English language.
- Knows that there are spaces between words.
- Knows a spelling pattern may represent different sounds.
- Knows the common spelling patterns in the English language.
- Uses serial probability of letters in a word. (There are possible letter

sequences in words in the English language, e.g., *amp* is possible, but not *jxm*.)
- Tries the 'does it look right?' strategy.

Morphemic
- Knows about using smaller words to spell compound words.
- Knows about adding prefixes and suffixes to base words.
- Knows generalizations about how to add suffixes to words.
- Knows that words in the same family will have the same spelling pattern (e.g., sign, signal, signature).
- Understands about using apostrophes for contractions.
- Understands about using apostrophes for possessive case.
- Uses knowledge about where the word came from — words from other languages, derivatives, eponyms, acronyms, portmanteau words, shortened words.

Can spell all the words you cant spell.
Can do words Just off the top of their heads in a second.
People dont have to correct their spelling as much as we do.
Some times were good Though
They know lots of words
Can read Better than us
Don't no how to spell all words
Can spell supercalafraglishceospelad

Ideas of a Year 2 child about good spellers.

A good speller:
- Can Sound out words
- reads a lot
- needs to know the alphabet
- goes to school to learn
- has a teacher to help
- practises a lot
- does not mess up words a lot
- knows almost every word
- thinks the words in their heads
- has good handwriting

These ideas about good spellers were provided by children at the beginning of Year 1.

A similar chart could be built up with students at various age groups by asking them what they think good spellers can do. This will be a guide to myths that may need to be dispelled, such as 'good spellers know how to spell everything' or 'good spellers never use a dictionary'. The teacher can contribute to the chart also but it should only include items that are achievable for those particular students. Such a chart could be referred to when the class or individuals are trying to think of how to spell a word and when students reflect on their own development in spelling. Further items can be added as necessary.

The teacher can select appropriate attributes to focus on depending on the understandings about written language displayed by students in their writing.

For example, if beginning writers are still just drawing or using scribble marks for writing it is not appropriate to begin exploring sound/symbol relationships. Even asking such students to try to spell by sounding out words may give them the idea that they do not know how to write because they cannot accomplish the expected skill. Such students need to see many demonstrations of letters being used to write words and need to be using letters in their own writing before the focus would shift to trying to represent sounds in any way.

Similarly, the exploration of generalizations about how to add suffixes to base words is not relevant until students have some idea about how to spell a body of words, and are able to read well enough to be able to recognize words in some type of word exploration.

The following ideas will assist in the achievement of these goals, particularly if the students also know what they are trying to achieve.

Attitude

As a writer's attitude to spelling affects students at all stages of their development, it is important for teachers to encourage positive attitudes and for students to have high expectations of themselves. The teacher should:

- Praise students' attempts at unknown words.
- Point out aspects that are correct or reasonable ideas about the spelling of words and allow students to notice the correct ideas they have in their attempts. The students may compare their attempts with the conventional form and tick each letter or part of their word that is correct.
- Demonstrate an interest in words and learning about written language.
- Encourage students to edit as much as possible for publication.
- Use assessment techniques that firstly focus on what the student *can* do and what progress is being made.
- Help parents to value what the students are achieving.

The teacher should not:

- Label students as failures nor designate students in fixed ability groups.

Habits

Similarly, habits that are characteristic of competent spellers should be encouraged as soon as possible but must be appropriate for each student's writing development. These include:

▼ *1 A system for learning new words*

When it is observed that students are consistently writing some words in the conventional form they may like to consider ways that help them remember what other words look like. One such technique is to:

LOOK at the word
SAY the word
COVER the word
WRITE the word
CHECK the word with the original
TRY IT AGAIN if it is not correct.

This technique is particularly useful when students are copying a word from another source. It is better to focus on the image of the entire word or parts of a longer word than to copy it letter by letter. It is also more useful for students to focus on meaning units if possible, such as parts of a compound word, or prefixes, suffixes and base words, rather than syllables, for example:

under/ground   mis/spell   commit/ment
yester/day   real/ly

Any word selected to learn must be recognized on sight by the student, its meaning must be understood and it must be a word that will be used in the student's writing. So this may not be a suitable technique to demonstrate until students are about six years old, although this will vary according to students' reading development.

▼ *2 Resources*

Many resources are helpful when trying to discover or confirm how a word is spelled. Writers need to develop an awareness of when it's appropriate to use a resource at the time of writing and when it's better to focus on recording ideas and to check resources later (especially for editing purposes). In general, it's more helpful to focus on content first, but there is no fixed rule about this because sometimes writers prefer to check a word at the time of writing it.

When students are first beginning to write it is better to encourage them to try words without asking how to spell them. Teachers need to be consistent about not showing students how to spell each word or the students will not develop the strategy of making an attempt first.

As learning how to spell involves problem solving, all students should be encouraged to attempt a word first, perhaps trying it several ways, and then to check with a resource. The *Have-A-Go* card is useful for this.

✿ Have a Go! ✿			
First try	**Second try**	**Third try**	**Correct**
neary	nearley	nearly ✓	nearly
wear	were	were ✓	were
ballayt	ballet ✓		ballet
tomoro	tomoreo	tomorrow	tomorrow
frinds	friends ✓		friends
steped	stepped	stepped ✓	stepped

The teacher has encouraged this Year 1 child by indicating which letters are correct in the first attempts. Assistance has been provided by rewriting the misspelled words and indicating where a letter is missing. If the child cannot spell the word the teacher can write the correct spelling in the final column.

Resources can be people or many kinds of print. On most occasions, when students ask someone else how to spell a word that person should first suggest that the writer make an attempt. Then the writer can be praised for whatever aspects are correct or make sense and then be shown how to spell the word. It is more helpful for the word to be written down, to provide a good visual image, than to be called out letter by letter. Sometimes a writer may have no idea how to attempt a particular word and it may not be wise to cause frustration. So be guided by the situation and knowledge of the student.

Print resources may vary from dictionaries or wordbooks to other books, magazines, newspapers, signs, charts or environmental print. The most important aspect for the writer to learn is to select the most appropriate resource. For example:

- The name of a city or town may be best located in an atlas, street directory, telephone book, post code book or zip code book.
- The name of a dog breed may be best located in a dog book.
- The name of a fellow student may be best located in a classroom list.
- A word being used in a current project may be best located on a class topic list.
- Many words may be found in dictionaries, thesauruses (e.g., *The Australian First Dictionary*, *The Australian First Thesaurus*) and wordbooks (e.g., *The Australian Writer's Wordbook*).

Provide a range of resources in the classroom, establishing a useful reference section in the classroom library. A range of types and levels of dictionaries should be included here, beginning with picture dictionaries through to some that give explanations of derivatives or other sources of words. Encourage students to select a dictionary that suits them for their own personal use at home and at school and discuss the importance of this with parents. Demonstrate how you would select and use such resources when you are writing and proofreading in front of or with the students and ask parents to do the same at home. This is the most relevant reason to introduce students to one of the major uses of dictionaries or wordbooks.

Students can be introduced to the following information about dictionaries as is appropriate for their writing development and ability:

- words are usually in columns
- words are in alphabetical order to assist in the location of a word — the dictionary begins at *a* and ends at *z*, and the words are also in alphabetical order within each letter section.
- words may be formed by locating a base word and adding other parts to the word
- words may be in other parts of a dictionary, such as appendices, introduction.

▼ *3 Memory aids*

Most people have difficulty remembering how to spell particular words and they devise something that will help overcome this. Although each writer needs to think of some link that is personally useful, there are many common ones that students may be interested in knowing about. As students learn about these and devise memory aids of their own they could make a class book for the reference section of the class library. Students may also like to record the ones they find useful in a personal spelling book (for more details about this refer to page 29). Many of the ways to remember which homophone to use correctly could be written about in a class homophone book, with illustrations or sentences to explain each word.

Memory aid book.

Some useful memory aids

Word	Memory Aid
separate	You are **a rat** (sep**arat**e) if you separate or you **part** (se**par**ate) when you separate.
piece	Have a **piec**e of **pie**.
quite/quiet	**Silent** ends with the letter **t** and **quiet** ends with the letter **t**.
here/hear	**Hear** contains the word **ear**.

there/their	Both words begin with **the** and the word **here** is in the word **the**re.
where/were	The word **here** is in the word w**here**.
two/too/to	**Two** is related in meaning to **tw**in and **tw**ice. **Too** means **also**. There is also another letter **o** or **more than** (more than one letter **o**).
currant/current	There is an **ant** eating the curr**ant** bun. So **currant** is the food and **current** is the flowing of the tide or river.
practice/practise	**Ice** is a noun, so pract**ice** is a noun and practise is a verb. (In American English, **practice** is used as both a noun and a verb.)
affect/effect	Think of the word RAVEN: remember, affect verb effect noun.
principal/principle	The princi**pal** is your **pal**.
stationery/stationary	You buy your pap**er** or **e**nvelopes in a station**er**y shop. The **car** was station**ar**y.
accommodation	There are two **c**aravans and two **m**otels.

Using helpful memory aids and referring to various resources will arise incidentally when the teacher is modelling writing or when it is noticed that students are having difficulty remembering certain words.

▼ *4 Proofreading*

When students are aware that they know how to spell some words in the conventional form they should be encouraged to proofread their writing to check that these words are correct. The more that students learn about spelling the more they should take on responsibility for proofreading and attempt to correct words that they think may be spelled incorrectly. Even at an early age students can check some known words. The important focus is to develop the *habit* rather that ensuring that the students correct *every* word. If some students were made to do this it would be so time consuming that they would be disinclined to write very much on future occasions.

A Year 1 child attempts to proofread and to correct her spellings. Circled words were thought to be wrong. The teacher has assisted after the words are circled by the child.

Not all pieces of writing need to be proofread and corrected and it is more suitable for students to select the pieces that they consider are worth spending time on, particularly if they are to be published. It should also be remembered that writers do not always identify their own mistakes, perhaps because they do not know the words are incorrect or because they are reading for meaning and just do not notice a mistake. It is helpful to have students proofread each other's writing and for someone to take on an editor's role before publication.

Show students proofreading techniques when they are able to check most of their own writing, for example, uncover writing line-by-line, using a piece of paper or a ruler. They could circle or underline words they think are spelled incorrectly and then try to find out the correct spelling for as many words as they can cope with. The students may use the *Have-A-Go* cards to assist with this process, by using the columns to attempt to correct words they think are spelled incorrectly.

▼ *5 Legible writing*

There seems to be a correlation between legible writing and competent spelling, although an illegible writer may be a good speller or a legible writer may be a poor speller. When writing is legible, particularly when a word is being copied from another source, it does provide a good visual image to remember what the word looks like. So it is helpful for students to adopt the habit of writing legibly. Students are best helped with individual attention for specific needs, such as the best ways to form and join letters.

Word knowledge

When students are starting to spell some words in the conventional way without needing to copy them, they are ready to begin to learn other words. The following ideas need to be included in the spelling program.

▼ *1 A developing body of words*

Students need to gradually increase the number and range of words that they know how to spell so that the words 'flow off the pen' with very little thought. These words need to be relevant to the writer's needs so each student should take personal responsibility for learning useful words. These will be different words for different students. A designated class list may have words that the student already knows how to spell or may not include words that the student most needs. Concentrating on a set list of words that the whole class or groups are to learn may be wasting the students' time. Although the teacher may specify some words to be learned, a system whereby students are making their own choices will be more purposeful and useful. Suggested ways to do this are described on pages 26-28.

▼ *2 Common words*

As the 100 most frequently used words make up about 50 per cent of our written language it is helpful for students to be able to spell them. These may be some of the designated words that a teacher suggest all students learn.

Words writers use			
a	it	but	she
the	sat	toys	see
to	and	next	then
I	in	do	will
at	said	run	he
him	for	little	had
you	big	all	take
was	have	finish	ran

Words suggested by Year 1 students as the most frequently written words.

A list of these arranged in alphabetical order is a useful chart. Students should assist the teacher to build up this list by observing which words most frequently occur in their own writing and in the material they are reading.

This class list could be compared with published lists of these common words, such as the one provided below. Some of the words will not be used frequently by some cultural groups and other words may be more relevant.

100 most commonly used words								
a	about	after	all	an	and	are	us	at
back	be	because	big	but	by			
came	can	Christmas	could					
day	did	do	dog	down				
for	from							
get	go	going	good	got				
had	have	he	her	him	his	home		
I	if	in	into	is	it			
just								
like	little							
man	me	morning	mother	my				
night	not							
of	off	on	one	our	out	over		
people	play							
ran								
said	saw	school	see	she	so	some	soon	started
that	the	their	them	then	there	they	this	three	time
to	too	two						
up	us							
very								
was	water	we	went	were	what	when	will	with	would
you								

Frequently used words arranged in alphabetical order.

When students are beginning to write some words in the conventional way and are willing to try to spell unknown words, they may find it useful to have some of the common words on a list in their writing folders or on their tables. They are not intended to be referred to so frequently that the flow of thought is interrupted but the list can be a resource.

If students consistently misspell a word for several weeks and think it is correct, it will eventually become harder for them to write it in the conventional way and to notice it when proofreading. This is more likely to occur with words they are writing frequently. Teachers could point out these mistakes as words for the student to learn. This idea should not be confused with that of encouraging the writers to experiment with spelling. Teachers need to be aware of each student's development.

When learning the high frequency words students should try to use other strategies that are more useful than rote memorization. It is more helpful if teachers include these words in other spelling exploration occurring throughout reading and writing sessions in all curriculum areas.

Example 1 The words may have the same spelling pattern as other words, for example, **could** and **would** have the same spelling pattern. Ask students to find other words with the same spelling pattern — sh**ould**, sh**ould**er, b**ould**er, m**ould** — and learn all of the words together. This is particularly helpful as the letter *l* is pronounced in many of the words, which reminds the students about this letter being in the other words even though it is not pronounced.

Example 2 From the list of common words look for words within words, to focus on the visual pattern, for example:

as in w**as**	Christ in **Christ**mas
ate in w**ate**r	out in ab**out**
hat in w**hat**	use in beca**use**

Example 3 From the list of common words find those that end in the spelling pattern *le*, for example, *little, people*. Ask students to search various resources to find other words with the same spelling pattern, such as *battle, settle, jungle, double, bugle, bungle, trouble, juggle, bubble, stumble, jumble, tumble.*

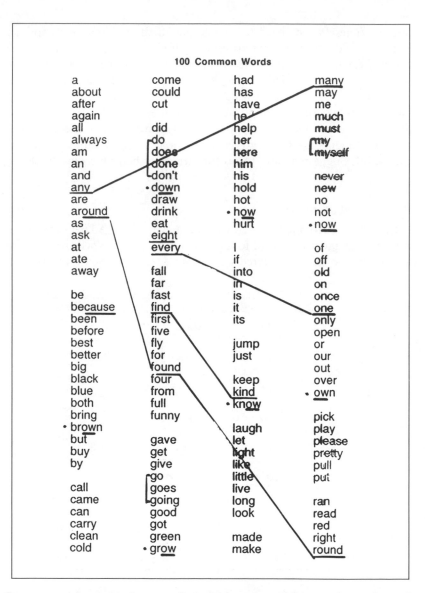

100 Common Words

a	come	had	many
about	could	has	may
after	cut	have	me
again		he	much
all	did	help	must
always	do	her	my
am	does	here	myself
an	done	him	
and	don't	his	never
any	down	hold	new
are	draw	hot	no
around	drink	how	not
as	eat	hurt	now
ask	eight		
at	every	I	of
ate		if	off
away	fall	into	old
	far	in	on
be	fast	is	once
because	find	it	one
been	first	its	only
before	five		open
best	fly	jump	or
better	for	just	our
big	found		out
black	four	keep	over
blue	from	kind	own
both	full	know	
bring	funny		pick
brown		laugh	play
but	gave	let	please
buy	get	light	pretty
by	give	like	pull
	go	little	put
call	goes	live	
came	going	long	ran
can	good	look	read
carry	got		red
clean	green	made	right
cold	grow	make	round

Some ways that a teacher may link the learning of frequently used words.

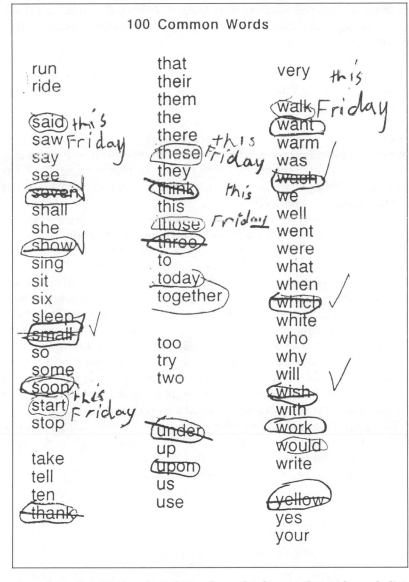

100 Common Words

run
ride
(said) *this*
saw *Friday*
say
see
~~seven~~
shall
she
(show) ✓
sing
sit
six
sleep ✓
~~small~~
so
(some)
(soon) *this Friday*
(start) *this Friday*
stop

take
tell
ten
~~thank~~

that
their
them
the
there
(these) *this Friday*
they
(think) *this*
this
(those) *this Friday*
~~three~~
to
(today)
(together)

too
try
two

(under)
up
(upon)
us
use

very *this*
(walk) *Friday*
(want)
warm
was
~~wash~~
we
well
went
were
what
when
(which) ✓
white
who
why
will ✓
(wish)
with
(work)
(would)
write

(yellow)
yes
your

A student chooses words to learn from the frequently used words list.

Students can continue to search for such words over several days. The words could then be regrouped according to other spelling patterns, for example:

| double | stumble | bungle |
| trouble | jumble | jungle |

Example 4   Use memory aids to distinguish between the use of words such as *their/there, where/were, to/too/two*.

Example 5   From the list of common words find words ending in the suffix *ed*, such as *started*. Include this in an exploration about how to add this suffix to words.

Example 6   When engaging the students in explorations of words with the same sound, include common words in the exploration, for example, words with the /i/ sound (as in *bite*) — *by, I, like, night*. Add other words with the same sound and regroup them according to the various letters or spelling patterns that represent that sound.

Example 7   When learning one of the common words think of other related words to learn at the same time, for example, *can — can't, cannot*.

Strategies

Although the English language is a morphemic language, at all ages people use visual, phonetic and morphemic strategies to help with the spelling of English words. (For more information about the English language refer to Chapter 2 of *Ideas for spelling*.) These strategies are not necessarily used in isolation from each other, but for some words one set of strategies may be more useful than another.

▼   *Using phonetic strategies*

To spell any unknown word that has not been seen before the writer may try to represent the sounds heard in the word. Beginning writers rely heavily on this strategy because they do not yet know a lot about written language. Experienced writers may use this strategy first and then try to apply other aspects they know about written language.

Example 1   The beginning writer who is aware of representing the sounds in a word may write the word *said* as S or SD or SED.

Example 2   An older writer who can apply many strategies may attempt an unknown word such as *phagocyte* as *fagosite* or *fagasite* or *phagasite*. Then they would apply knowledge about its meaning (a special type of blood cell), decide the spelling is more likely to be *phagocyte* (because other science words end with *cyte*) and then use a dictionary to check the correct spelling.

▼   *Using visual strategies*

Sometimes the writer remembers what a word looks like, or will try a word several ways and then decide which way looks the best. Sometimes they will recognize particular visual patterns of letters and know that some are acceptable patterns in the English language but others are not. They may know that a particular word is likely to have the same spelling pattern as another known word.

Example 1   To spell the word *cake* the writer may think of the spelling of words such as *take* and *bake* and presume it will have the same spelling pattern and then possibly check with a dictionary or wordbook.

Example 2   To spell the word *misspell* the writer may think that *mispell* looks better than *misspell*, but another strategy will need to be applied, such as adding a prefix to a base word (*mis/spell*).

▼   *Using morphemic (meaning) strategies*

Example 1   To spell a word such as *somebody* the writer should use knowledge about the spelling of *some* and/or *body* and realize that a compound word will have the same spelling because it has the same meaning base.

Example 2   To spell words such as *unnecessary* (*un/necessary*) or *commitment* (*commit/ment*) the writer should use knowledge about adding prefixes or suffixes to base words.

Example 3   To spell words such as *hopped*, *budgeted*, *carried*, *troubled*, *panicked* the writer should use knowledge of generalizations about how to add suffixes to base words.

Example 4   To spell words such as *pasteurization* the writer should apply knowledge about how the word was derived. In this case it is from a person's name (Louis *Pasteur*).

Example 5   To spell words such as *mortgage* the writer should apply knowledge about how the word was derived. In this case it is from the root *mort* meaning *death* (*mortgage* originally meant *dead pledge*). So it has the same spelling pattern as other words based on that derivative, such as *mortuary*, *mortal*, *mortician*.

Details of what students could learn about the phonetic, visual and morphemic aspects of the written language and how to apply those strategies are provided in Chapters 5 to 11. The resource lists are comprehensive but do not contain every possible example. As you become aware of additional examples add them to the appropriate list. This does not mean that every prefix, suffix, derivative, etc. should be learned. The way this knowledge can assist with spelling is the most important thing for students to learn and the approach to that learning should encompass the following ideas.

• The focus should relate to the students' writing at that point in time.
• The students should not be given the information as a statement of fact to memorize, but they should investigate many examples and form a hypothesis that is constantly reviewed and refined.
• The students should express what they have learned in their own words.
• The students should reflect on how this learning will help them to spell other words and therefore help with future writing.

For specific examples of this approach see pages 21-23.

Class Explorations
and Student Responsibilities

3

Class explorations

To build a community of learners who are interested in written language, many aspects of spelling can be explored as a class. The goal should be to learn about the language rather than just to learn a list of words. If students learned 20 words per week for five years at school they would only know how to spell approximately 4000 words and that will not be sufficient for their writing needs. However, if they can apply knowledge about the language to any word they wish to spell they will have more power over their writing.

When students first begin school the emphasis is on encouraging them to write and all of their attempts to do so are valued. They will invent many ways to spell as they gradually progress towards conventional spelling and details about this progress and ways to enhance it are outlined in *Ideas for spelling*.

Class interest in the spelling of words is greatly influenced by what the teacher personally models, how writing demonstrations occur throughout the day and the opportunities and purposes students have for writing. From the time when students show in their own writing that they are starting to use letters in an organized way to represent words, class explorations can commence.

It is preferable for some learning about spelling to take place for 10–15 minutes each day. That might occur in any curriculum area, whether planned or incidental, with the class, groups or individuals. The following ideas may be appropriate for the class.

Daily word focus

One way to do this is to select a word a day that students may be interested in and encourage different students to attempt to spell the word throughout the day. Meet with the class to look at the various attempts and ask some students to share their ideas about how they attempted the spelling. In doing so, the students become aware of the different strategies being used. Circle the correct spelling if it exists or show the students ways to work out how the word is spelled.

Word for the day

pewn
penwen
penwin
penwyn
pengwin
penwon
pennwinn
pengwen
penguin

Some of the Year 1/2 attempts to spell **penguin**.

A student using magnetic letters to attempt words.

The strategies demonstrated will vary with different age groups. This type of activity could begin with the use of a picture of something that the students try to write the word for, but this would limit the words to noun types. So also progress to words in sentences, where one or more of the words is deleted as in a cloze task. The sentence should be read first with the missing word(s) being pronounced and then students begin their spelling attempts. A special notice board could be used for this each day, placed somewhere that all students can reach.

A magnetic board and magnetic letters could also be placed near this task so that students have the opportunity to try various letter combinations before they write the word. This magnetic board could be available for students to attempt any words they wish to try.

This daily word activity should extend with older students to such ideas as:

- Write other words with the same spelling pattern.
- Write other words by adding prefixes and suffixes.
- Write compound words, using this word.
- Write other words with the same derivative.
- What words does this acronym stand for?
- Who was this word named after?
- Make a compound staircase, starting with this word.
- Find these words in this maze.

(Refer to chapters 5–11 for any other possibilities.)

Incidental learning

There are many instances throughout the day when either a student or teacher notices something about the spelling of a word and the more this occurs in all curriculum areas the better. This may remain just a short discussion or it may lead to a class exploration over a number of days.

For example, a first grade teacher was writing the daily class journal with her class and a student noticed that the word *supermarket* was made up of two words, *super* and *market*, so the teacher mentioned that this was called a compound word. Another student then noticed another word of this type, *meatballs*. The class wanted to look back through previous days' journals to find others and the teacher listed them. The students continued to search for other compound words at home and at school so the list grew over several days. The important spelling point to help the students was that if they knew how to spell one word it could help them with related compound words, for example:

supermarket → **Super**man, **Super**girl, **Super**woman, **Super** Bowl
super**market** → fruit **market**, craft **market**, **market** garden.

The students could look at the list of class compound words and then try to spell other related words. To keep a record of what they have learned, and so that it can be accessed for future writing, a class book of compound words could be made, with a page for each letter of the alphabet. This resource could be placed in the writing area or class library and added to at any time. The teacher should model how to use this resource on future writing occasions so that the students realize its relevance and also refer to it.

Wednesday, September 16
Lilly went to the supermarket with
her grandma, her mother and her
younger brother. They bought
spaghetti and meatballs for dinner.
Mmmm!

Compound words
supermarket (A.A.)   oatmeal (R.L.)
meatballs (S.W.)   Batgirl
grandma (J.C.)   Batwoman
see saw (C.T.)   Superwoman
grandpa (H.Z.)   snowball (S.W.)
schoolbag (S.W.)   Batman
newspaper (S.W.)   Superman
peanut (A.L.)
afternoon (R.L.)
breakfast (A.A.)   Teacher: May Mui,
                              P.S. 42,
                          Manhattan NY

Writing this daily class journal grew into a search for compound words.
(Initials in brackets are students who provided the words.)

Planned class learning

The teacher can also plan one or two aspects about spelling as a focus each week, based on what has been observed in students' writing. This planning can focus on any of the attitudes, habits, word knowledge and strategies that are listed in Chapter 2 and include any of the ideas outlined in Chapters 5–11, but it should definitely be related to the students' knowledge about written language. The objective should be to extend students' learning, based upon what they already know and to provide them with a range of strategies.

It is likely that the focus with early writers will be on visual and phonetic strategies. This will change to more of an emphasis on morphemic strategies as the students' knowledge of language develops. If the focus is recorded in a teacher's work plan the teacher can continually reflect on whether there is a balance of strategies being dealt with.

Although Chapters 5–11 provide fairly comprehensive lists of words in various categories, it is not necessary to deal with every sound, spelling pattern, compound word, prefix, suffix, derivative, and so on. It is necessary to help students understand how learning these aspects of the language can help them to attempt to spell any word. The lists are not complete and students or teachers could add to them.

Although the focus should be related to the students' writing, the class reading should be used as a resource for language exploration.

One such scenario may be when a teacher notices that the grade one students are attempting to represent the sounds they hear to try to spell words. The class could explore the various letters or letter groupings that can represent one of the sounds, for example, the /ee/ sound:

- Select some of the words the students are trying to write that contain this sound and write their attempts on a chart. Say the words and discuss the fact that they all have this sound. Students may like to suggest various ways that they think their words could be spelled.
- Choose something that the class has read and reread it, asking the students to listen for any words with the /ee/ sound, for example, *monkey, tree, be, see, believe, seize, mean, he.*
- List the words and identify the part of each word that represents the /ee/ sound.

- Ask the students if they know or can find any other words with the /ee/ sound. They could write these on separate cards or strips of paper. Add them to the class list.
- Regroup the words according to their spelling patterns:

monkey   tree   be   believe   seize   mean

           see   he

     Alternatively the students could be asked to work in small groups with their word cards to see if they can find various ways to group the words. Share these ideas and discuss how they can be grouped according to their spelling patterns.

- Refer back to the original words the students were trying to write and ask if the students have any new ideas about how they could be spelled. If necessary show the students how to spell some of the words.
- Ask the students what they have learned that could help them with spelling in the future.
- Perhaps continue to add to the list of words with this sound during the next few days as students locate other words from their reading and writing.
- A class book could be made that groups words according to their sounds. A section for each sound in the English language could be allowed for and as other sounds are explored the relevant words would be added to those sections.
- Ensure the link is made with students' writing by encouraging students to check with this list when proofreading their writing or to use this knowledge to attempt words in their future writing.
- Students may also wish to learn some of these words and record them in their own Sound Spelling Books (refer to page 29).

     Another scenario may be when the teacher notices that the students are writing words of the type where it would be useful for them to explore a generalization such as how to add the suffix *ed* to a base word. Or one of the students may notice that there is a difference between the spelling of something such as *hop* and *hopped*.

- Choose a story that the class has read and reread it, asking the students to search for any words ending in *ed*, for example, *hopped, croaked, cried, skipped, watched, tried, snuffled, nestled, benefited, blossomed.*

cried = _cry_ + _ed_

tried = _try_ + ed

marry + ed = _married_

hurry + ed = _hurried_

worry + ed = _worried_

bury + ed = _buried_

carry + ed = _carried_

A word ending with y that you want to add _ed_ — you change y to _i_ and add _ed_. In other words when the y goes away the _i_ comes to stay.

*A student adds the suffix **ed** to words ending in **y** and writes a generalization in own wording.*

- List the words with the base word:

  hop — hopped, croak — croaked, cry — cried,
  skip — skipped, watch — watched, try — tried,
  snuffle — snuffled, nestle — nestled, benefit — benefited,
  blossom — blossomed.

- Ask the students what they notice about the way the base word has changed when adding *ed* and regroup the words according to the different types of changes:

croak — croaked	hop — hopped
watch — watched	skip — skipped
benefit — benefited	
blossom — blossomed	
snuffle — snuffled	cry — cried
nestle — nestled	try — tried

- Ask students to write (in their own wording) general statements about what to do if adding *ed* to different types of words. Compare the way different students have expressed these. Ask students to continue to find other *ed* words to add to the list during the next few days and to refer to these statements to check if they hold true.
- Ask students how this information could help them with their spelling in the future.
- Students could keep a spelling journal (refer to page 29) in which they record this kind of information to refer to for future writing. A class resource book could be made of *ed* words, with separate sections for each of the types of changes made to the base word before the *ed* is added. This should be kept with dictionaries and other resources used to confirm spelling.
- Ensure that the link is made with students' writing by encouraging students to check such words when proofreading.

Another way to build interest around a particular focus is to begin a class chart placed somewhere that others in the school could contribute

to. For example, if the class is investigating words with the prefix *un* the students' words could be listed and the chart placed on the classroom door so that other people could add such words. The students would need to check the meaning of any unknown words and then make statements about what they have learned.

Whenever there is a class focus a list of related words and information should be recorded on a chart and/or in a book so that the learning is synthesized. This also provides a reference for future writing and is a model for students recording information in their personal spelling journals. (See page 29). The teacher may suggest that students choose some words from the class list to include in their personal learning for that week.

Topic or theme lists

When students are investigating a theme or topic a list of related words may be developed and these could be a resource for students' writing. Such words could also be used to focus on aspects of the written language for spelling. Again the emphasis would vary for different age groups, and the main intention is to explore the patterns or organization of the language. The following examples show the possibilities that could arise with a list of topic words, but only a few should be selected as jumping off points for a class focus.

▼ *Grade 2 investigation about weather*

Topic words: storm   rain   thunder   lightning   rainbow   flood
snow   clouds   sunny   wind   drizzle   showers
frost   raincoat   ear-muffs   gloves   hat
drought   sun hat   block-out   scarf   temperature
frozen   overcast   weather bureau

Possible spelling focuses:

• words with the /oh/ sound (as in the word *go*)
sn**ow**   rainc**oat**   fr**o**zen   bur**eau**   rainb**ow**   **o**vercast
(Add other words students know with the same sound and identify the different ways to represent that sound.)

• words with the /u/ sound (as in the word *up*)
th**u**nder   fl**oo**d   gloves
s**u**nny
ear-m**u**ffs
s**u**n hat
(Add other words students know with the same sound and identify the different ways to represent that sound.)

• compound words
rainbow   raincoat   ear-muff   sun hat
block-out   overcast   weather bureau
(Identify the parts of each word and write other words that contain one of the word parts, for example, sun hat → **sun**bake, **sun** glasses, **sun**shine, **hat**-band, **hat** shop.)

• words with the *er* spelling pattern
thund**er**   show**ers**   overcast   temp**er**ature   weath**er**
(Add other words students know with the same spelling pattern.)

▼ *Grade 4/5/6 investigation about weather*

Topic words: storm   rain   thunder   lightning   rainbow   flood
snow   clouds   sunny   wind   drizzle   showers
frost   blizzard   high   low   pressure system
moisture   humidity   climate   evaporation
precipitation   condensation   turbulence
moderate   velocity   northerly   southerly
easterly   westerly   mercury   prediction
forecast   Celsius   Fahrenheit   meteorology
rain gauge   cold front   atmosphere   smog

Possible spelling focuses:

• compound words
rainbow   pressure system   rain gauge   cold front
(Identify the parts of each word and write other words that contain one of the word parts, for example, pressure system → **pressure** group, nervous **system**, **systems** analysis.)

• words that are eponyms
Celsius   Fahrenheit
(Students investigate the origin of these words.)

• portmanteau words
smog
(Students investigate the origin of this word — **sm**oke + **f**og.)

• words with the suffix *ly*
norther**ly**   souther**ly**   easter**ly**   wester**ly**
(Find other words with this suffix and note how it is usually just added to the base word. Compare with these directional words where *er* is added to the base word before adding the suffix.)

• words with the *tion* suffix
evapora**tion**   precipita**tion**   condensa**tion**   predic**tion**
(Add other words students know with the same suffix. Discuss the pronunciation /**shun**/ and compare with other words students know with the suffix *tion*.)

- build word families
  predict — predicting, predicted, predicts, predictable, unpredictable, predictability, prediction

- words with derivatives
  atmosphere, **veloci**ty
  (Students investigate meaning of derivatives and find other words based on same derivatives.)

Class journals and written conversations

The writing of a class journal is one way to model many aspects about writing for the students, including form and style, content, punctuation and spelling. It is a valuable piece of shared writing for the class and individuals to read and reread on later occasions as a memory of class or individual events. This can be written by the teacher, and individual students can be encouraged to participate in the writing. Their spelling attempts should be valued. When such journals are reread later in the year the students are usually surprised about the way their spelling has improved if they have been allowed to do the writing. In this way the journal becomes a form of assessment of the students' progress.

C	I went to dimau yesterday there were 1,000,000,000,000,000 people going crazy over the **orsome foursome** .
T	I heard about the awesome foursome going to Daimaru on the radio yesterday morning. Did they sign lots of autographs?
C	They sined lots of autogaphs every one was in a queue.
T	Did they sign an autograph for you?
C	NO I could not be bothered to wait ten hundred hours and I did not have any time to get a autograph.
T	Tell me what you did in Daimaru.
C	I got some cloths and that was super boring but when we were walking back I went in to a games shop and bought the dynasound then daimaru gave me a birthday present.

Written conversation between a teacher (T) and a Year 4 child (C) while working on a computer. They also discussed the homophones **or** *and* **awe** *and the suffix* **some**.

In a similar way the teacher and students can share in a written conversation where the teacher may write a statement or question and one of the students replies with a question or statement. This provides opportunities for the teacher to model the words the students are writing and so give positive feedback on any spelling attempts.

Written conversation between the teacher and a Year 1 child. Note the change in the spelling of the word **parties** *after the teacher has demonstrated how it is spelled.*

Student responsibilities

Writing conferences and proofreading

When teachers assist individual students and small groups with spelling needs during writing conferences, it is useful to look at a number of pieces of a student's writing to try to determine some common or frequent problems. Then the teacher can focus on areas of need, rather than just help the student correct words in his/her writing. Students should then be encouraged to take on certain responsibilities to improve their own spelling competency by deciding on something they need to learn more about.

When the writing has already been proofread, teachers can meet with their students to discover what range of strategies are being used for self-correction. This will provide a better overall picture of what the student knows about spelling and what may be the most suitable thing to focus on next. Teachers will find that some students have similar needs and so they could be gathered together for a group discussion or demonstration. Some aspects may be a general need for most of the class and so the teacher could choose this as an area for class exploration or demonstration.

A teacher will not be able to meet with each student to review every piece of writing. This does not matter when the emphasis is on learning habits and strategies rather than just learning words. It is better to spend some quality time with each student less frequently than to meet more often and only have time to correct individual words.

As students learn more about this process and about ways to collaborate with each other in pairs or small groups the teacher should not be seen as the only source of assistance. Every student in the class is good at something, whether it be roller-blading, knowing about dinosaurs, remembering the words of songs or being further advanced in spelling knowledge. All of these skills need to be recognized and shared with the class so that every student is seen as a resource for others who need ideas, information or help with a task. In such a co-operative environment there is no harm in students deciding who they could go to for help with spelling, particularly at the proofreading stage.

Individuals learning words

As competent spellers have a body of known words that they want to use for their writing, it can be helpful to instigate some system of students selecting certain words to learn each week. These need not be the same words for each student as it is wasteful if the words are already known by some individuals or if they are not words that an individual wants to use for personal writing. Each student can select a number of words useful for his or her writing and partners can test each other at the end of the week. They need not select the same number of words although a limit could be set so that students are more intent on selecting what will be most useful and what they can achieve success with.

Base Words
Rain — Rainbow rainstorm
rained raining
school playschool schools school
play (played) plays playing
plays playground
Open Opens Opening Opener
Keiko Keiko's Keiko Kamuta

A student selects own words to learn and then uses those as base words to build other words.

The students could select words at the beginning of the week and test each other in pairs at the end of the week. It is not necessary for partners to be able to read each other's words. It is interesting how they help each other with this task. Students should not view this as a 'test' in the traditional sense of the word, but rather a way of finding out about their learning. It could be called a 'trial' or something else to eliminate the element of competition. The *number* of words correct or incorrect is not the important issue. (Refer to page 37 for more details.)

The teacher can guide the choice of words if necessary by helping students locate words they are frequently using, but misspelling, in their writing. Also, the class may be investigating a particular theme or topic or be involved in writing about some common issue, and a related class word list may be developed on a chart as a reference for the students' writing. The teacher may indicate that students should select words from such a list as part of their learning at that point in time. As usual the students need to choose words they do not already know how to spell and words that they think will be useful to know.

Teachers who are used to giving spelling pre-tests may find that the following plan could be of benefit to the students:

1 The topic list should be developed with the students.
2 Tell the students that you could assist them to find out which words they know how to spell and which ones they are not sure of.
3 Cover the word list and read out each of the words while the students try to write them.
4 Allow students to check which words they have spelled correctly.
5 Tell students to select some to learn that they did not spell correctly. They need to make choices according to criteria such as:
   • the words that would be most useful for their writing
   • the words they are capable of learning
   • the number they could learn at one time.

These words would then be included in the student's personal list of words to be learned.

The students should try to apply the various strategies they know to help remember the words rather than just try to learn them by rote. This will be influenced by the types of spelling explorations teachers are engaged in with the class. If the students are not able to spell some of their chosen words when tested by a partner they should consider whether or not these words would be useful to retain for the next week's list and if so, what other

strategies they may use to help remember them. When students know how to spell a word they have chosen, they could also think about how this knowledge would help them to spell other words. For example:

how → bow cow low mow now row sow tow wow

like → liked liking likes dislike disliked dislikes likeable alike unlikely (same word family, adding prefixes and suffixes)

fairies → dairies hill-billies berries lorries (same generalization applied, changing the *y* to an *i*)

some → somebody something somewhere (compound words containing the base word)

medic → medicine medical (same meaning base)

This exercise will vary with different age groups, depending on how much they understand about the written language. If the students are required to do spelling homework this would be a useful homework activity.

When students think of other words they should check the spelling in some type of resource.

▼ *A class routine for learning words*

One possible class routine for students learning personal words could be:

1 During the week each student keeps some type of record of the possible range of words that could be learned. These should be related to writing needs and may be words from sources such as class lists, books being read, environmental print or personal writing pieces. The student and the teacher may be involved in these choices, with input from the teacher being most useful when he or she notices that a student is frequently using particular words incorrectly and would be capable of learning them. The words could be recorded in a book or on a card in the student's writing folder. Someone who is a competent speller needs to write or check the words to ensure that the words for learning are spelled correctly. This is more easily done if the recording is occurring throughout

the week rather than every student needing words checked at the one time.

2 On Monday the student selects appropriate words to learn for the coming week.

3 Assign a few minutes each day on Tuesday, Wednesday and Thursday for the students to refer to their words in ways that will help to learn them. For example, students could be thinking about how to:

- write rhyming words and check their spelling in a dictionary or wordbook
- look for words within words and write them
- think of other words with the same spelling pattern, write these and check their spelling in a dictionary or wordbook
- use the words to write compound words
- change words into plurals if possible
- add prefixes and suffixes to the words to write as many other words as possible and check these in a dictionary or wordbook
- find the derivative of the words if possible and write other words with the same derivative
- think of memory aids to help remember how some words are spelled and share these with the class
- use the LOOK, SAY, COVER, WRITE, CHECK strategy to remember some words.

This task will vary according to the students' stage of writing development. They could also organize the words into spelling resource books such as those described later in this chapter. They may like to make word games to play with their family or classmates. (Ideas for such games may be found in Chapter 11.) If homework is a requirement, any of these would be suitable homework assignments and would be more useful tasks than writing the words several times or writing the words in sentences. When usage is important, such as which homophone is appropriate, then writing the word in a sentence is worthwhile. Apart from this writing words in sentences is not a worthwhile spelling activity — rather it is a vocabulary activity. It is also unnecessary for spelling because students should know the meanings of the words they are learning.

The teacher may engage the entire class in the same activity each day, even though the students will have different words. Depending on what the students know about spelling, the teacher might ask them to do tasks such as:

- look at your list to write any of the words that have a particular feature, such as, any words that begin with the letter *m*
  any words that contain the /**ee**/ sound
  any words that have a double letter
  any words that are compound words
  any words that contain a prefix or a suffix.

Or the teacher might specify tasks such as:

- write the plural of one of your words
- use a word to make a compound word
- add a prefix or suffix to a word to make a new word
- write other words that these words would help you to spell.

4 On Friday the students can 'test' each other in pairs. Partner A reads aloud the words of partner B while partner B writes them and then vice versa. They then either check each other's spelling or check their own spelling; checking one's own is more useful for the student's learning.

Each student should then think about what they have learned about spelling that week and how this will help their writing, record that learning in some way (which could be in the spelling resource books described below). Words not learned could be included in the list for the following week if the student still considers such words to be the most useful.

Students could also test some of each other's words from previous weeks to allow for feedback about whether these words are retained.

5 At a class meeting or in groups, ask students to share some of the general knowledge about spelling they have learned.

A variation on the above procedure would be to have a different group of students select their words each day so that there is a chance to check that the words are spelled correctly. This would also mean that the 'testing' would be done by a group each day. Another variation is to follow the process during a two-week period.

Personal spelling journals or resource books

The students may like to keep a record of the words or information they are learning in spelling journals or personal resource books and refer to this personal record when proofreading their writing. If they do keep a record it needs to be easily accessible so students should consider whether they will organize the words according to their first letter or some other way that makes sense to them. Such journals that have a cumulative list of known words and known information about spelling can be a record for the student to reflect on his or her development and can be part of the portfolio used for assessment.

A suitable progression of the type of spelling journals or resource books for students is outlined below. A number of these groupings could be kept in the same book. There is no point in introducing any of the ideas until the students' writing and knowledge of language indicates that they are ready to compile and use such resources. Nor should students be keeping more than one type of these personal spelling resources unless they find them particularly useful and interesting. There may be some types of whole class books being kept while individual students just organize their learning in one type of book. The main goals are to help students understand the organization of the English written language by synthesizing class explorations as they relate to their personal words, and to provide them with resources that they find personally useful for their writing. There is hardly any point in asking the students to keep such spelling journals if they are not encouraged to refer to them to check or confirm spelling.

▼ 1 Words I know how to spell

This could simply be a card or page that is kept in the writing folder. It is good for the self-esteem and self-evaluation of beginning writers for them to realize that they do know how to spell a number of words consistently in the conventional way. The teacher helps to establish such a list for each student by looking through a number of pieces of the student's writing with the student, and indicating which words are spelled correctly. Then the student or the teacher writes the words on the student's personal *Words I know* list. During future writing conferences other words can be added. Such a list should be a point of reference for the student when proofreading.

A Year 1 child writes the words that she knows how to spell. When children list their own words in this way the teacher can provide feedback by indicating the ones that are not correct.

▼ 2 Alphabet spelling book

When the list of known words becomes too long for the student to easily locate words, there is a reason for organizing them in some way. A spelling journal with a double page spread for each letter of the alphabet could be introduced. Students could look at class alphabet lists and decide whether they need to allow more pages for words beginning with some letters of the alphabet and less for others.

▼ 3 Sound spelling book

Another way for students to organize words is to group them according to a sound or sounds in each word. As there are 44 sounds in the English language a book could be divided into 44 sections, with a table of contents for easy location. A list of the sounds can be found on pages 57–59.

Allow at least a double page spread for each sound so that words can then be grouped according to the various spelling patterns for each sound. For example:

/oo/ (as in 'book')

oo	oul	u
took	would	push
cook	could	cushion
brook	should	bush
crook		
shook		
looking		

The students may list the words they have selected to learn and other words they are interested in. They may find they will continue to add other groups to each section as they discover other ways to represent sounds. Two students may list the same word in a different place if they pronounce the words slightly differently; this is bound to occur because there are many dialects of English. The word placement in the book must be relevant to the students if they are to easily locate the words again.

A word could also be placed in more than one section, if the student wished to do so. For example, the word *muddy* could be placed in the following sound sections:

/m/ muddy	/d/ muddy
/u/ muddy	/ee/ muddy

▼ *4 Spelling patterns book*

Another way for students to organize words is to group them according to a spelling pattern or patterns in each word. As there are many different spelling patterns in the English language a book could have a table of contents for easy location and this could be added to as students enter new words. A list of spelling patterns can be found on page 48. Words could be grouped according to the various sounds for each spelling pattern. For

example, these words with the **ea** spelling pattern are grouped according to their sounds:

bread	bead	great
read	read	
dead	eaten	
	treat	

A word could also be placed in more than one section, if the student wished to do so. For example, the word *springboard* could be placed in the following sections:

ing	spr**ing**board
oar	springb**oar**d

oo spelling pattern

took, hook, book, crook, look, chook, foot, football, "woof", brooke, Brooke, bookshelf, cook, good, wood, wooden

cool, pool, fool, school, tool

food, spoon, roots, soon, zoo, kangaroo, baboon, choose, boomerang, afternoon, room, bathroom, bedroom, food, too, loo, "Boo"

Pooh Bear, "Ah-Choo", bamboo

flood, blood

brooch

An example of an /oo/ spelling pattern chart.

WORDS WITH "th" AT THE BEGINNING		WORDS WITH "th" IN THE MIDDLE		WORDS WITH "th" AT THE END	
the	thumb	I'd rather be skiing!		mouth	
those	thermometer	Dorothy		earth	
them	over there	Bathroom		moth	
that	their house	godmother		bath	
Thursday	they're yummy	godfather		hearth	
things		healthy		length	LENGTH
thunder		wealthy		width	WIDTH
this		clothe		cloth	
thank		clothes		month	June
thanks		clothing		Meredith	
thank you		clothed		tooth	
than		weather		teeth	
three 3		leather		death	
third 3rd		Maths 12+3=15		with	
thirty		Mathematics 12-9=3		fourth 4th	
thief		Katherine		fifth 5th	
theft		birthday		sixth 6th	
think		toothbrush		seventh 7th	
thinks		toothpaste		eighth 8th	
thinking		without		ninth 9th	
thought		author		tenth 10th	
throat		other			
thong		Mother			
theatre ticket	ADMIT ONE	brother			
over there		father			
thin					

Page from a child's spelling pattern book showing where the spelling pattern **th** *occurs in words.*

▼ *5 'What I have learned about spelling' book*

As the focus moves towards the morphemic strategies for spelling it would be more useful for the students to be recording what they are learning in categories other than alphabetical, sound grouping or visual patterns. Such categories could be:

- Homophones (with a sentence or illustration to explain correct usage)
- Compound words
- Contractions
- Apostrophe for possession

- Prefixes
- Suffixes
- Generalizations
- Derivatives
- Acronyms
- Eponyms
- Portmanteau words
- Word families

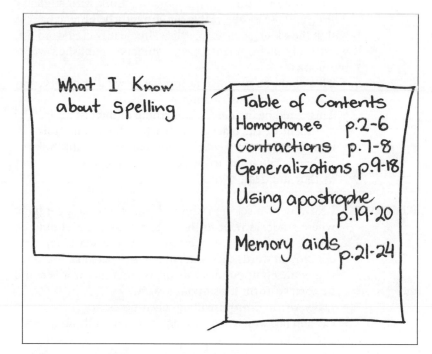

What I Know about Spelling

Table of Contents
Homophones p.2-6
Contractions p.7-8
Generalizations p.9-18
Using apostrophe p.19-20
Memory aids p.21-24

Spelling resource book.

A book or loose-leaf folder could be divided into sections, with a table of contents and words or information recorded as the students learn about these. They may continue to add to or refine their recorded ideas, particularly about generalizations. This personal resource is one that the student may use for a number of years.

Combining class explorations and students' individual work

The general plan for a period of one or two weeks could be as follows:

Class Focus on one or two aspects of spelling to explore and allow a short time for this daily, if possible. Link with students' writing and use resources that are currently being read or exist within the room, such as topic lists, frequently used word list, word wall, environmental print, students' published work, big books.

- This could be planned, according to what is observed as a need in students' writing.
- This could be incidental; something of interest noticed by a student or the teacher. (If teachers have some form of mandated requirements for the year, they could look for authentic situations to introduce them and check them off as they are dealt with.)

Individuals
- Learning own selected words. A short time is spent daily where students refer to these. The class focus should be linked with these, for example, if the class focus is compound words each student refers to personal list to see if any are compound words or to see if any words could be used to form a compound word.
- Daily writing, proofreading when necessary.
- Conference with teacher as required, hopefully about once per week.

If the class focuses are recorded in a work plan, the teacher can continually reflect on whether the students are being introduced to a range of spelling strategies and habits. With younger students there will tend to be more focus on phonetic and visual strategies. With older students there should be more focus on morphemic strategies.

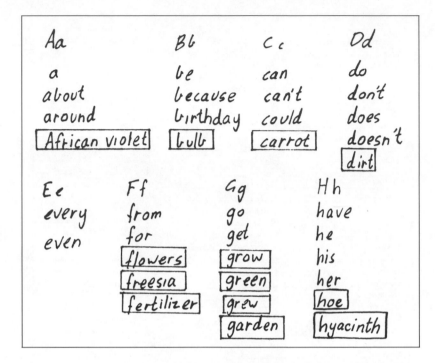

Section of a word wall, with high frequency words and topic words (on cards) that can be removed to make a topic book. Words are referred to as part of word searches relating to class focus. Students may select some of these words for personal learning.

Summary

The chart on the following pages is a summary of the development of class and individual spelling activities that are detailed in the preceding pages. The chart demonstrates the connections between the class explorations and individual responsibilities within a spelling program. Although it starts with activities for beginning writers and progresses in general to those suitable for more experienced writers, not all activities will occur in such a lock-step manner. Some activities will occur over many grade levels and sometimes more than one activity will occur at the same time.

Year Level	Class/Teacher	Individuals
K-all grades	Demonstrate writing in front of students, e.g., class journals, signs, notices, letters, recounts of experiences, recipes, lists, observations, etc. This provides different purposes for writing and therefore a reason to learn about writing. This also develops concepts about print and understandings about the meaning of *word* and *letter*, the use of upper and lower case letters, and spaces between words. (Note: This demonstration should continue at all grade levels, focusing on strategies used to attempt and then check words, how to use various resources, how to proofread, etc.)	Students are encouraged to write for various purposes and audiences. This may begin with drawing and/or writing forms such as scribble, symbols, letters and invented spelling. This provides opportunities to explore concepts about print, gradually developing understandings about words and letters.
K	Model purposes and forms of writing by reading aloud to the students and engaging them in shared reading experiences. This also provides information about the concepts of print and knowledge about words and letters.	Students are given opportunities to read independently and to join in with shared reading and to locate particular words.
K-all grades	Through reading and writing experiences encourage an interest in and recognition of words. Focus on recognizing high frequency words in particular.	Students become interested in words, recognizing some, e.g., own name and words of personal interest.
K-1	Teach alphabet names in context of all print being read and written. Develop alphabet friezes, charts and books for each letter name.	Students help to find words for each letter of the alphabet. They may make their own alphabet cards, charts, friezes, books.
K-1	Explore the idea that each letter may represent more than one sound.	Students could look for such words in their own reading and writing.

Year Level	Class/Teacher	Individuals
late K-1	Encourage students to assist with the spelling of some words and to attempt to write some of the class journals, signs, etc. Provide other situations to encourage an interest in attempting words, such as magnetic board and letters and a word a day for various students to try to spell before it is compared with the conventional form. Develop the idea that a good speller tries to spell unknown words.	Students are willing to attempt unknown words in their writing. To encourage this teachers do not usually spell students' words for them, but in some circumstances this may occur.
late K	Develop a class list of commonly used and recognized words. Add to this as other words are known. Refer to other print as resources for spelling.	Students are writing some words the conventional way and have personal 'Words I know how to spell' lists to be used for checking spelling. Can begin the habit of proofreading but will not be able to self-correct all writing.
late K	Known class words could be organized as an alphabetical word wall, where words are placed according to their first letter. Continue to add to this. Introduce picture dictionaries.	Students could organize personally known words in personal alphabet wordbooks and add to this as other words are known. This is to be used when proofreading writing.
1	Encourage students to remember how to spell some words. Begin a system to allow for this, perhaps starting with some students who are ready.	Students begin to select some words to learn, with some guidance from the teacher if necessary. They test each other to check their learning.
1	Begin to explore the sounds of the language, discovering that each sound may be represented by various letters or spelling patterns. Develop charts and books for the sounds.	Some students may want to organize their words into personal sound books, with different columns for each spelling pattern.
late 1	Introduce homophones as being those words with the same sound but different spelling. Develop class chart or book of homophones with artwork to indicate meaning.	Students may want a section for homophones in their personal spelling books.
1	Continue to find out which words are most used in writing and add these to the word wall. Topical words can be added on a temporary basis and removed when no longer needed. These could be organized into class books of topic words for future reference. Introduce easy dictionaries and wordbooks.	Students may have personal copies of the most used words to refer to when writing and to choose from for learning words. Students also use dictionaries, wordbooks and other class resources for checking some words.

Year Level	Class/Teacher	Individuals
1	Begin to explore spelling patterns in words and regroup according to pronunciation.	Students refer to personal words to find those with spelling patterns being explored. They try to build other words based on the same spelling patterns as those in their personal lists.
late 1	Explore compound words and how each part of these may be used to build new words. Build class charts as students find others.	Students refer to personal words to build compound words if possible. They may choose some compound words to learn.
late 1	Explore contractions and their meaning. Build class charts as students find others.	Students may choose to learn some contractions they are using in their writing.
2	Words on word wall could be reorganized within each letter column to introduce more specific alphabetical order. Show the relevance of this when using dictionaries, wordbooks and other alphabetical resources.	Students may want to reorganize some of their own lists in alphabetical order for easier location.
2	Discover generalizations about how to form plurals. Write statements and lists or books about this and about the following explorations. Introduce a variety of dictionaries.	Students begin a personal Spelling Resource Book to record information they are learning about the various focuses being explored. They refer to this and revise as necessary. They also use personal words they have selected to learn and write other words based on these, e.g., by adding prefixes or suffixes. They reflect on how this knowledge will help them with their writing. Students take on more responsibility for proofreading. They should select a dictionary to suit personal needs and value owning one. This may not be the same one for each student and a student should consider acquiring more sophisticated dictionaries as the need arises.
3	Explore adding prefixes.	
3	Explore adding suffixes; discover generalizations about these.	
4,5,6	Explore derivatives, use of possessive apostrophe, acronyms, eponyms, portmanteau words, proprietary names, words from other languages.	

Assessment

4

It is important to select a range of assessment procedures. Some will give immediate feedback for the students about their strengths and needs (for directing their current learning and informing the teacher's planning). Others will demonstrate the longer term growth of students' spelling ability.

For immediate feedback to the students include:

- observation and analysis of current writing and proofreading
- peer testing of personal word lists
- attempts on *Have-A-Go* cards
- questionnaires about what is being learned related to the current class spelling focus.

For the demonstration of long term growth include:

- questionnaires about the students' personal views of their spelling ability
- re-editing of earlier pieces of writing
- testing of the same words after a lengthy period
- analysis of the information students record in their personal spelling journals or resource books
- comparison of students' writing at various times of the year.

Teachers need to select various assessment procedures to satisfy the needs of different clients: students, the school or system and parents. For example, students will gain most from the above procedures, but the school or system might demand a specific or standardized test. Parents may want to see the results of both informal and formal assessment, but they will learn more about their child's strengths, needs and development from informal assessment.

Teachers should plan which procedures they will use to satisfy the demands of all three clients, decide how often each type needs to be used and reported on, what will be the most useful and manageable way to record information and who should keep such records. They should encourage students to take responsibility for as much as possible.

There are also several ideas for assessment, evaluation and record keeping presented in *Ideas for spelling*, Chapter 7.

Questionnaires

Provide students with questionnaires about their own spelling. These would vary according to the development of the students' writing. The questions will also be an indication of what you value about your students' spelling.

Am I a good speller? – Example 1

I write often. ....

I read often. ....

I am willing to attempt unknown words. ....

I know how to spell some words. ....

I am learning how to spell other words. ....

I try to proofread my writing. ....

I try to use resources to check my spelling. ....

I am interested in words. ....

I know that nobody knows how to spell every word. ....

<table>
<tr><td colspan="2">

Am I a good speller? – Example 2

I write often. ....

I read often. ....

I sometimes notice how words are spelled when I'm reading books and other printed material. ....

I proofread my writing when it is going to be published in some way or when it matters to the reader. ....

Sometimes I have others proofread my writing. ....

I care about being a good speller. ....

I use various strategies to try to spell different words. ....

I use various resources to check the spelling of words. ....

I am learning about the way the English written language works.

I know how to spell the most frequently written words. ....

I have a systematic way of learning new words. ....

</td></tr>
</table>

Throughout the year students may like to rate themselves between low and high on each of the above points to see if they are making progress and to note areas that they need to work on.

Re-editing

When students are proofreading and editing their own writing one form of assessment is to ask them to return to a draft of some writing done several weeks or months earlier and to re-edit it. The students should note what they have learned in that period of time. This should include not just words that they now know how to spell but also knowledge about the written language that they realize they have gained. Teachers can assist students to make comparisons as they may not be aware of all of the things they have learned. Some pieces of writing could be kept in a special file for this purpose. When the writing is first analyzed the students could make a list of what they know about spelling and then add to this list on subsequent occasions.

Pre and post publishing review

Students could also look at a piece of writing before and after editing and publishing to review how much they are able to do themselves in relation to proofreading and using various strategies and resources.

Comparing development with selected words

At the beginning, middle and end of a school year teachers may like to use a specific list of words for all students to attempt to spell. Each student's development can then be assessed by comparing their attempts at the different times. The words can be selected to suit the age group. For example, words with different spelling patterns may be chosen for young students but the words could include elements such as plurals, derivatives, affixes, and so on for older students. If teachers work in a school system where there is set content to be covered at particular grade levels and more formal testing is required, this could be one way to satisfy the needs of the system and also provide useful data about the students' development. Assess this by looking at the range of strategies the student is using to attempt words and how close these approximations are to the conventional patterns of the English language.

Word	Student's attempt early in year	Student's attempt middle of year	Student's attempt end of year
RED	R	RD	RED
MAN	M	MEN	MAN
BIT	BT	BET	BIT
CUP	K	CP	CUP
JOG	G	JOG	JOG
KITE	KT	KIT	KIT
YOU	U	YU	YOU
ZOO	Z	ZOW	ZOO
FACE	F	FS	FAS
THREE	R	THREE	THREE
GO	G	GOW	GO
SHADOW	SH	SHAO	SHADO

Here is an example of a student's spelling attempts in Year 1.

Analyzing spelling errors

Even when students are tested with the same set of words it is important to look at the type of error(s) being made and to assess how close the words are to possible English spellings. One student may be misspelling more words than another, but may exhibit more understanding of English spelling. And two students who spell the same words wrongly may need quite different assistance with spelling.

The following example shows how three students spelled the same set of words. Student 1 has spelled more words correctly, but the misspelled words indicate a lack of knowledge of possible English spelling. Perhaps this student is just able to rely on a good visual memory for the weekly test that was given in this class.

Words	Student 1	Student 2	Student 3
cake	cake	cake	cake
circus	ciusis	circs	cricus
cents	cents	cens	cents
corn	corn	corn	corn
circle	cielel	circl	cerkal
cap	cap	cap	cap
candle	candle	candel	candle
central	central	cetryl	cenchral
could	could	could	could

The type of spelling mistakes each student makes are varied and it would be necessary to look at writing samples to see if there are any patterns emerging that may relate to spelling pattern knowledge, pronunciation, reversal of letters and so on. A numerical assessment provides insufficient information about these students' spelling ability.

Reviewing the class focus

To help teachers and students to review what has been learned by individuals a simple task is to ask a question related to the spelling focus for that week.

Example 1 If the class has been exploring the suffix *ed* ask the students 'What have you learned about the suffix *ed*?'

*A student's generalization for adding the suffix **ed**.*

Example 2 If the class has been exploring the suffix *ing* ask the students 'What have you learned about the suffix *ing*?'

*Another student's generalization about adding the suffix **ing**.*

This assessment procedure could be used orally with young students, but when they are able to write answers it helps them write their way into a better understanding, to revise and refine what they are writing, to have a written record of what they are thinking — a record that can be referred to as further learning takes place. It enables the teacher to have some idea about how clear or confused the students' understandings are and to use this information for further teaching or refining with groups or individuals. It should be remembered that a student may not be able to explain something but may well be able to use the knowledge in their writing. So this procedure should only be coupled with actual observations of students' writing.

Evaluation

A teacher or parent evaluation checklist could also be used to reflect on ways the learning environment is influencing the students' attitudes, habits and skill development. The following questionnaire could be used to do this.

Questionnaire: Learning conditions for spelling

Place a tick in the space if you facilitate your children's acquisition of written language in the following ways:

My children are surrounded by print being used for many real purposes. ....
My children know I value reading and writing. ....
My children see me read frequently. ....
My children see me write frequently. ....
My children see me attempt to spell unknown words. ....
My children see me use dictionaries and other resources to confirm my spelling attempts. ....
I expect my children will write just as I expected they would talk. ....
I expect my children will eventually spell conventionally, knowing that this does not occur as soon as they begin writing. ....
I value my children's attempts in spelling. ....
I appreciate what they can already do. ....

I am interested in the content of my children's writing and not just the spelling. ....
I respond positively to my children's attempts to spell unknown words. ....
I do not usually correct my children's misspellings, unless I am being the editor to help them when they request assistance. ....
I sometimes show them how to spell the words they are using in their writing and compare the similarities and differences between their spellings and the correct ones. ....
I encourage my children to spell a word as best as they can before I assist them. ....
My children choose the words they want to learn. ....
My children want to write. ....
My children believe they can write. ....
I provide plenty of paper, pencils, etc. for writing. ....
I provide a place for my children to write. ....
I provide time for my children to write. ....
My children write for real purposes and audiences so there is a reason for learning how to spell. ....

If these conditions are not being met at school and at home then they should be addressed as much as possible.

Exploring Sound/Symbol Relationships

Letter names

Students should first be taught letter names so that they have a consistent label for each letter even though letters may be pronounced different ways in different words.

The following is a list of the letters of the alphabet and the various sounds they may represent. It is not intended as a list of words to be learned.

a   was above fat water any acorn naive last
b   lamb birthday
c   ice ocean cat cello
d   dentist soldier
e   wet entree pretty debut
f   of father
g   go giraffe
h   honor happy
i   ski in medicine meringue find Australia
j   jump
k   kite
l   like walk
m   many
n   nothing
o   dog women do one front photo
p   pneumonia pretty
q   quick liquor
r   ran
s   dogs sugar seven leisure
t   tonight listen nation creature
u   cut bury business use push language lieutenant
v   very
w   went lawn
x   fox xylophone
y   yellow very syrup type
z   zebra

Points to think about

Points to consider when students are learning about letter names include:

▼   *Letter combinations*

In the list above letters were not included when combined with other letters, such as *c* with *h* to form *ch* or *p* with *h* to form *ph*. If students suggest words that contain such combinations, for example, *cherry* or *photo*, they should be accepted and the letter being focused on underlined. The combined letters (*ch* and *ph*) and the sounds they represent could be briefly discussed.

▼   *Understanding the difference between a letter and a word*

Ensure students understand what the term *letter* means by using the term in various contexts, such as finding the number of letters in their names and in the titles of books.

▼ Contexts for learning letters

Learning about letters should be done within the context of students' reading and writing. It is important that students are involved in shared reading experiences using big books, poem and song charts and other environmental print so that learning about letters can occur using words that children recognize in their reading.

▼ Exploring the sounds represented by a letter

The name of a letter remains constant, but a letter may represent many different sounds, these being determined by its position in a word and the surrounding letters. For example, the letter **a** does not always represent /a/ as in *cat*. The letter **a** also represents the:

/o/ sound in **was**
/u/ sound in **above**
/or/ sound in **water**
/e/ sound in **any**, and so on.

It is important to give students accurate information about the sound-symbol relationships in the English written language. They can actually become confused when they are told that *a* is /a/ as in *cat* and then they encounter the letter *a* in other words where this information is incorrect.

▼ The difference between a letter's name and the sounds it represents

It is incorrect to talk about a *sound* when you really mean a *letter name*. For example, the letter *g* is not the sound /g/ as in *goat*. It is misleading to present activities with confusing information about letters and sounds, as shown in the following activity.

'Circle the words that belong with the sound *g* (pronounced gee).'

There is a letter *g* but not a sound *g*. The letter *g* can represent more than one sound (as in *goat* and *giraffe*). A suitable activity is to find words that students know the meaning of that begin with or contain the letter *g*, such as *goat* and *giraffe*, *ago* and *age*.

▼ Observing students' knowledge about letters

Find out which students in your class recognize the names of the upper and lower case letters so that you know who needs help with this in small group or individual work.

Also observe which students are using letters in their writing so that you know which students are aware that words consist of letters. Through discussion find out if these students can accurately name the letters they are using. This is important because some students may recognize letters but may not be able to accurately use them in writing. Involving the class in activities that help them learn about letters can enhance students' willingness and ability to use them when writing.

Provide students with an alphabet strip of upper and lower case letters to refer to when writing. Assist them to identify and locate letters they wish to use. Picture cues are not necessary and may confuse students because the word for the picture will only represent a limited range of possible sounds for the letter.

▼ Teaching about letter names that are relevant to students' writing needs

There is no particular sequence in which letter names should be learned. Learning names in alphabetical sequence is irrelevant. It is more pertinent to focus on a letter that is occurring in many words the students are reading at that time. For example, if the class is referring to the word *March* for journal writing it may be appropriate to focus on the letter *m*. Although there may be a class focus each student may learn some letters that are more personally important, such as the letters in their names.

▼ Spelling words orally

If orally spelling a word letter names must be used. Sounds could be represented by many letters so it is not useful to just indicate sounds.

▼ Inexperienced writers using letter names when writing

Using letter names is a strategy inexperienced writers use when attempting to spell unknown words, for example, *R u rede*? (Are you ready?) When students start to analyze a word into its sounds they tend to match a sound with a letter name that is the same as the sound.

▼ *Recognizing letters in a variety of typefaces*

Both capital letters and lower case letters need to be learned. Introduce students to a variety of print styles, so that they recognize the various forms of letters. Students have no difficulty in recognizing individual letters in various typefaces. A series of alphabet cards could be made with the various forms of each letter.

a a *a* A A *A*
b b *b* B B *B*

Research has found that young readers get used to a variety of type faces. They find it no more difficult to identify *a* than a or even A. Once students discover that these shapes all represent the one letter they quickly become familiar with them and perceive them without difficulty as the same letter.

Activities

The following activities can be used to help students learn about letter names:

▼ *Using literature as a model for students' writing*

Read alphabet books to the students (see Resources, page 57) and make multiple copies of class alphabet books. Place these in the library so that the students may borrow them to read with their parents. Refer back to these books as each letter is explored with the class.

▼ *Developing class charts*

Develop a series of charts, one for each letter of the alphabet. Initially focus on letters in the initial position and as students become more confident also consider letters in the middle and final positions of words.

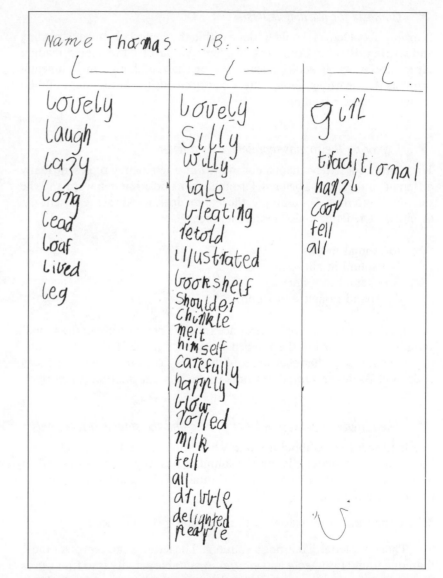

A Year 1 student classifies words according to the position of the letter l in the word.

Allow the students to cut out or draw pictures of objects or people. Write a label for each picture and talk about the names of the letters in each word. Assist the students to highlight a letter in the label (at first the initial letter) and to place their picture on the appropriate letter-name chart. Display these charts around the room at a height the children can easily see and refer to.

Note: Once students have a body of words they recognize, words only may be listed, showing letters in various positions in words. Not all words can be illustrated.

▼ *Learning about a particular letter*

Choose a letter to focus on, for example, the letter *c*. With the students reread a familiar big book or class chart asking the students to look for words containing the letter *c*. Also ask students if any of their names contain the letter *c*. Saying these words together, write the words on a chart. For each different sound that the letter *c* represents begin a new column. For example:

ice	caught	ocean	Christine
circle	circle		Michael
icecream	icecream		
cent	crack		cherry
city	picnic		
circus	circus		Cheryl
cereal	caterpillar		
	cave		

Note: The words with the *ch* spelling pattern would be included because the students will notice that these words contain the letter *c*. They could be grouped separately, with discussion about the sounds formed when the letters *c* and *h* are combined.

Underline the letter *c* in each word and once students are familiar with the procedure encourage individuals to locate and underline the letter in each word.

Talk with the students about how the letter *c* may be pronounced in different ways. Some words may be listed more than once, for example the words *circle*, *circus* and *icecream* because the letter *c* represents more than one sound in these words.

Ask the students to search their class charts, topic lists, alphabet books and other reading materials for words containing the letter *c*. All words that the students understand that contain the letter, regardless of the sound represented by it, should be included on the letter *c* chart. Over the next few days continue to list other words containing the letter *c* in the appropriate columns.

▼ *Publishing alphabet books*

As the students learn each letter name assist them to publish a big book with a page for each letter or a small book for each letter of the alphabet. These could consist of pictures cut from magazines or students' illustrations. Ensure that where appropriate students include artwork demonstrating the variety of sounds a letter represents. It is also important that students realize

The letters being focused on here, b *and* c, *occur in various positions in the words. The letters* b *and* c *also represent different sounds in the different words, for example, the letter* c *in* **circus** *and* **cat**.

that letters occur in different positions in the words, not just the initial position. Therefore include words in which the letter name being focused on occurs in the initial, medial and final positions.

Discuss with the students alphabetical order and suggest this as being a useful way of organizing the letter name big book. A contents page could be included for easy reference. The big book could be placed in the class library for the students to refer to or borrow. Talk with the students about how knowing the names of the letters of the alphabet will assist them when writing. Demonstrate the use of such books by referring to them when writing with the students and encourage the students to refer to them for their personal writing.

▼ *Using published materials as models for students' writing*

In areas that are easily seen and referred to display commercial alphabet friezes in the classroom and publish class alphabet friezes. Refer to the friezes regularly. Talk with the students about the letter that comes before *c* and the letter that comes after *h*, and so on. Talk with the students about how knowing about alphabetical order will help them locate a letter on their letter strip when they are writing.

▼ *Creating a word wall*

Create a word wall, with a section for each letter of the alphabet. Begin the wall by selecting high frequency words that the students recognize and place them in the appropriate alphabet section according to the first letter of each word. Involve the students in deciding which are the high frequency words they notice in their reading and use most often in their writing. Encourage them to find the appropriate section to place each word.

For topics or themes that you study, write related words on cards and add to the appropriate section of the word wall. These words may change depending on the topics that students are writing about. The words that are removed may be used for word games or made into a topic word book.

If all words are written on cards older students could place them in alphabetical order in each letter section and continue to do this as new words are added.

Part of the word wall that has a section for each letter of the alphabet.

▼ *Using picture dictionaries to learn about letter names*

Collect a variety of picture dictionaries and place them in the class library. When studying a particular letter name refer to these dictionaries and compare the entries. Encourage the students to browse through these and borrow them.

▼ *Developing charts with content in alphabetical order*

Develop class charts, for example, students' names, pets, streets, that are organized in alphabetical order to demonstrate the usefulness of this form.

Students' names	Students' pets	Street names
Alison	budgerigar	Alice St.
Fatima	cat	Ellis St.
Georgie	dog	Feather St.
Keiko	horse	George St.

Various charts organized in alphabetical order assist students to learn the usefulness of this form.

As the students acquire more pets, change addresses, and so on, it will be necessary to alter the chart. To facilitate this it may be useful to write the names of the pets, streets, and so on, on cards and attach them to the chart with Blu-tack. In this way it will be easy to alter the chart in order to maintain alphabetical order. Talk with the students about how knowing about alphabetical order will help them with their writing.

▼ *Using alphabetical order to locate information*

Introduce the notion of being able to locate information using letter names and alphabetical order. For example, make a class telephone directory or a class dictionary or wordbook. Talk with the students about how knowing about alphabetical order will help them with their writing.

Note: If it is a dictionary the words entered should have artwork, related sentences or definitions that indicate the meaning of the entry. If words are simply listed in a book in alphabetical order and the meaning of the word is not indicated, it is a wordbook.

▼ *Sorting, matching and naming letters*

Provide sets of cardboard, foam and plastic letters or magnetic boards and letters for the students to play with. Use them for sorting and matching activities requiring the students to group the same letters together. Students must name each group of letters.

▼ *Alphabet jigsaws*

Make alphabet jigsaws in the shape of snakes, worms, lizards, and so on. The pieces join together in alphabetical order. If necessary, encourage the students to refer to alphabet friezes, class charts, picture dictionaries, alphabet strips, and so on. The students must name the letters after they have put the jigsaw together. Talk with them about how knowing about letter names will assist them when writing.

An alphabet jigsaw.

▼   *Teaching letter names using alphabet rhymes, poems and songs*

Teach *names* of the letters of the alphabet using alphabet poems, rhymes and jingles that contain both lower and upper case letters. The students can also dramatize some of the poems. For example:

> *A   was an Ant,*
> *B   was its Brother,*
> *C   Caught it,*
> *D   Drew it,*
> *E   Eyed it,*
> *F   was Frightened of it,*
> *G   Got it,*
> *H   Had it,*
> *I   Inspected it,*
> *J   Jumped over it,*
> *K   Kept it,*
> *L   Left it,*
> *M   Moved it,*
> *N   Nodded at it,*
> *O   Ordered it,*
> *P   Peeped at it,*
> *Q   Quickly touched it,*
> *R   Ran for it,*
> *S   Sat on it,*
> *T   Tickled it,*
> *U   Upset it,*
> *V   Viewed it,*
> *W   Won it*
> *XYZ   all wished for an ant of their own.*

A class chart could be made of each alphabet poem and these could be displayed in the classroom. A class big book of alphabet poems and jingles could also be made, with multiple copies of a smaller version. The students could borrow these and take them home for their parents to read to them and for them to read with their parents.

The class could also write its own alphabet poem about an object. For example:

> *A   was an Alligator,*
> *B   it took a Big Bite,*
> *C   it was Colored*
> *D   it Drank water . . .*

Here is a different type of alphabet rhyme that could also be used as the basis of substitute writing activities.

> *A, B, C, D, E, F, G,*
> *I see a kookaburra in a tree.*
> *H, I, J, K, L, M, N,*
> *The kookaburra flew away again.*
> *O, P, Q, R, S, T, U,*
> *It came back and said 'How do you do?'*
> *V, W, X, Y and Z,*
> *Now I must go, it's time for bed.*

> *A, B, C, D, E, F, G,*
> *I see a cockatoo in a tree.*
> *H, I, J, K, L, M, N,*
> *The cockatoo flew away again.*
> *O, P, Q, R, S, T, U,*
> *It came back and said 'How do you do?'*
> *V, W, X, Y and Z,*
> *Now I must go, it's time for tea.*

Note the variation in the last word in the final line in the two poems above, *bed* and *tea*, to allow for variations in the pronunciation of the letter *z* — /**zed**/ and /**zee**/.

A, B, C, D, E, F, G,
Then H and I and J
Are letters of the alphabet
I practise every day.
K, L, M and N, O, P
and Q, R, S and T
Along with U, V, W
And finally X, Y, Z.

Students need to be able to identify specific letters, so be sure to point to each one during reading, with students watching carefully. After the reading ask individuals to locate a specific letter, using its name.

▼ *Naming letters – Hop Scotch*

Play games with alphabet tiles, for example, Hop Scotch. Place the cards on the floor. The students name the letter as they land in it.

▼ *Naming letters – Snap and Bingo*

Card games such as Snap and Bingo can be played. Various sets of cards could be used for these games, including sets of upper case letters, lower case letters and words (with pictures) that begin with a particular letter. Initially it may be useful to have some sets of cards the same as the alphabet friezes and alphabet books in the room. The students can then refer to the friezes and books to check that the letters and words they have do match. Ask the students to think about how knowing the names of the letters of the alphabet will assist them when writing.

▼ *Playing 'I Spy' with words that begin and end with particular letters*

Throughout the day play *I Spy* where students say *I spy with my little eye something beginning with . . . (Letter name).* As well as saying the letter name the students can also pick up the letter from a set of plastic letters and display it for the class to see. The students then try to identify what the object may be.

A class *I Spy* book could be made with a page for each letter of the alphabet. To add interest, a cardboard magnifying glass with a cellophane 'glass-piece' could be used with the book and the students could use this when saying *I spy with . . .* Students take turns in *spying.* A more difficult variation of this game is to play *I spy with my little eye something that ends with the letter . . . I spy* can also be played with picture dictionaries.

▼ *Playing games with blocks to learn letter names*

Play games using blocks with letters written on them. Here are some ideas.
• A player rolls a block then names the letter on the top of the block and has to find an object in the classroom that begins with that letter.
• A small group of students roll some blocks to see if they can make a word from the letters.
• Two sets of blocks are used — one with upper case letters of the alphabet and one with lower case letters. The sets of blocks are arranged in two groups on the floor. A player picks up one upper case block and one lower case block. When the same upper and lower case letters appear the player wins a point. The player with the most points wins.

The students will also create many games of their own. Talk with the students about how knowing the names of the letters of the alphabet will assist them when writing.

Spelling patterns

A spelling pattern is a group of letters representing a sound. On page 48 is a list of common spelling patterns.

Each spelling pattern listed represents more than one sound, thus encouraging learners to actively explore the sound-symbol relationships that exist in the English written language. Where a common spelling pattern represents only one sound, it has been included in the Common Sounds section on pages 57–66. For example, the spelling pattern *sh* only represents the /**sh**/ sound, as in *ship*, unless it is placed between two syllables, as in the word *mishap*. For this reason the spelling pattern *sh* is not listed in this section but is listed in the /**sh**/ section of the common sounds, together with other words containing the /**sh**/ sound, for example, *machine* and *tissue*.

In the following list of common spelling patterns, the only double letters listed as spelling patterns are those that represent more than one sound, such as *oo*, *ee* and *cc*. This is to encourage students to actively explore the sound-symbol relationships that exist. Double letters that represent only one sound appear under the common sound that they represent, for example, *tt* is listed under the /**t**/ sound.

This list is provided as a resource of the range of spelling patterns and the varieties of ways they may be pronounced. It is not intended as a list of words to be learned.

ai	plait plaid aim said Thailand naive
amp	damp swamp
ant	plant want
ar	car war various around arid
are	bare are
arm	warm farm
as	has was
at	hat what
au	author gauge aunt chauvinist
augh	laugh caught
cc	cappuccino vaccine broccoli succinct flaccid
ch	champagne cherry yacht monarch choir
ea	bread eat great create
ear	earth bear heart near nuclear
eau	beauty plateau
ee	seen entree
ei	seize forfeit reindeer leisure neither
eigh	height weigh Leigh
eir	weird heir Eire
eo	people leopard surgeon video
ere	were here

ew	sew new jewel blew
ey	key prey eye
ie	thief sieve pie friend view mischievous experience
ind	window find
oa	broad road
oe	shoe does amoeba poet goes
ome	some home welcome
one	done bone one
ong	among strong
oo	soon look flood brooch
or	for world orange doctor
ose	nose whose
ost	lost most
oth	moth other
ou	found country group bouquet
ough	cough enough through thought plough
ould	could mould
ound	found wound
our	yourself tour courage hour courteous
ove	move drove glove
ow	now flow knowledge
own	down owner
ss	tissue toss possess
th	with then Thailand
ua	usual language
uar	guard guarantee January
ue	Tuesday guess glue cruel colleague
ui	guide build fruit suite guitars genuine nuisance
umb	thumb number
ush	bush rush
ut	cut put

Points to think about

Points to consider when students are learning about spelling patterns include:

▼ *Introducing spelling patterns*

There is no point in dealing with spelling patterns until the students have a body of words they recognize and they know the names of the letters, so that they have the language to talk about the letters in the spelling pattern. It is also important to consider the development of students' oral vocabulary to ensure they understand the meanings of many words with the same spelling pattern.

▼ *Teaching about spelling patterns that are relevant to students' writing needs*

There is no particular sequence in which spelling patterns should be studied and they do not all need to be studied. The purpose of studying spelling patterns is to raise students' awareness of the visual aspect of the written language and how being familiar with common patterns will help them remember the possible spelling of words. Those students require for their personal writing needs are the spelling patterns that should be dealt with at any given time. It may be that a spelling pattern is studied on more than one occasion in a particular year level, and it may be that the same spelling pattern is also studied again in subsequent years, depending on the writing needs of the students. If a spelling pattern is studied on more than one occasion it is likely that in doing so the words being considered will be different words.

▼ *Looking for spelling patterns*

It is important to give students clear, consistent instructions and to ensure they understand that they *look* for spelling patterns. Initially it may be useful to wear a pair of cardboard glasses to cue students into looking for a pattern. In this way they will not confuse looking for spelling patterns with listening for common sounds.

*A pair of cardboard glasses can remind students to **look** for spelling patterns.*

▼ *Learning about the possible letter sequences in the English written language*

It is vital in a spelling program to develop a variety of class word lists and to draw attention to them as a reference for writing. Class lists that focus on visual spelling patterns assist learners to understand which letter patterns can occur in the English written language. For example, the word *mip* could exist in the English written language as it follows the same pattern as words such as *hip*, *rip* and *zip*. However, a word such as *ctp* would not occur because it does not follow a conventional pattern. The English orthography predictably has a vowel in every word in order to make letter strings pronounceable. Similarly, you would expect to find patterns such as *ear*, *tion*, *orn*, *ame*, *ough* and *dge* but not patterns such as *ij*, *inb*, *amd* and *iul*.

Class lists should relate to students' writing needs and may be developed from students' personal writing, class or group topic work, class or group reading or writing activities and individual wordbooks. There is no point in providing a list of words that students do not know the meaning of nor have any use for in their writing.

When students discover spelling patterns class lists can be developed like those shown here. Underline the spelling patterns and discuss how the spelling pattern can represent a variety of sounds.

▼ *Teaching spelling patterns and common sounds exclusively of each other*

If focusing on a spelling pattern and a common sound in the one week try to keep them exclusive of each other until the students fully understand that they *look* for spelling patterns and *listen* for a common sound. For example, if exploring the spelling pattern *ch* do not study a sound that is related to the spelling pattern *ch*, such as /**k**/ and /**ch**/.

Activities

The following activities can be used to help students learn about spelling patterns:

▼ *Developing class lists*

As students discover spelling patterns when reading or when they begin using them in their writing start a class list of words for each spelling pattern and encourage them to add to the list as they find others. When listing words with a common spelling pattern ensure the students understand their meanings and that they are words they are likely to use in their writing. Ask the students to underline the spelling pattern in each word and talk with them about what a spelling pattern is, ensuring that they understand it is a group of letters that exist in the English written language.

Using words from the class spelling pattern list demonstrate to the students how the spelling pattern can represent a variety of sounds. Ask the students to think about how knowing this will help them when attempting to spell unknown words in their writing.

When selecting a spelling pattern to focus on, choose one that will be most useful for the students to know about for their personal writing. Here is an example procedure for exploring any spelling pattern.

Spelling pattern *ough*
Ask the students to search their personal writing, class charts, topic lists, lists of common words, word wall, and reading materials for words containing the spelling pattern *ough*. All words that the students understand that contain the pattern, regardless of the sound represented by the spelling pattern, should be included. For example, if studying the *ough* spelling pattern, words such as *though*, *cough*, *through* and *enough* should be listed if the students understand the meanings of these words.

cough	though	tough
brought	trough	dough
sought	draught	rougher
roughly	toughness	wrought
roughness	through	thoroughly
enough	rough	bought
bough	thought	although
fought	nought	roughest
tougher	toughest	ought
throughout	thorough	

*Class list of words containing the spelling pattern **ough**.*

The spelling pattern could be underlined in each word. Talk with the students about how the spelling pattern, in this instance *ough*, does not always represent the same sound. As the class list develops ask the students to group the words so that those with the same sound are together.

'ough' spelling pattern

bough   enough   though   aught   trough
drought   taught   dough   naught   cough
rough   although   sought
rougher   wrought
roughest   bought
tougher   brought
toughest   thought
toughness   fought
roughness
roughly   throughout
thorough   through
thoroughly

Students in Year 3 regrouped the **ough** *words according to the sound* **ough** *represents.*

Repeat this procedure with other spelling patterns relevant to students' writing needs. Ask the students to think about how knowing about common spelling patterns will help them when attempting to spell unknown words in their writing. When the wall charts are no longer displayed use them to make either a big book of spelling patterns or a small book for each spelling pattern.

▼ *Students selecting words to learn*

Some of the words students select to learn may contain a spelling pattern, for example, *ie* in the word *thief*. It is useful to list other words that contain the same spelling pattern for students to learn, for example, *pie*, *friend*, *sieve* and *view*. Although time consuming it is important that teachers or very competent spellers enter the words to be learned, especially in the initial stages. If students enter the words it is essential that they are checked by the teacher to ensure they are spelled conventionally.

It is also useful to list words where the spelling patterns represent a variety of sounds. Ask the students to think about how learning other words with the same spelling pattern will help them when they are writing.

▼ *Students creating activities for others to complete*

It may become apparent during discussions with students or from reading their writing that further clarification of their understandings about spelling patterns is necessary. If this is so, students could complete activities similar to the following and could also create such activities for their peers to complete. The words selected for the activities should be taken from class lists, students' writing and reading materials, lists of words they have selected to learn, topic lists, a list of commonly used words, and other sources that are relevant to them.

1 Word searches

A word search involves students in searching through written materials (both published and students' own writing) for words containing, in this instance, a particular spelling pattern. Sometimes when searching for a spelling pattern, for example *ou*, the students will find words such as *could* and *through*. This is not incorrect since the spelling pattern *ou* does occur in these words. However, because *ould* and *ough* are spelling patterns in their own right it is appropriate that these spelling patterns be dealt with separately. You may write the words *could* and *through* at the time the students suggest such words but isolate them as separate groups that could be dealt with in relation to other words with the spelling pattern *ould* and *ough* respectively. Talk with the students about how knowing about spelling patterns will assist them when writing.

2 Crosswords and mazes

Crosswords may be developed in which all the answers contain a particular spelling pattern. Similarly, word mazes may be developed that focus on a single spelling pattern. If possible use computer software such as *Crossword Magic* and *Super Wordfind* (see Resources, page 57) to develop crosswords and mazes.

Across

2 Time when you have tea.

5 A group of players. Rhymes with scream.

Down

1 Clean and tidy. Rhymes with feet.

Across

6 To find out the size of something. Rhymes with pleasure.

10 . . . . . , set, go! Rhymes with steady.

12 To make something new.

13 When we have good health we are . . . . The opposite of unhealthy.

15 Used for sandwiches, rhymes with dead.

16 Corn, wheat, rice and other grains used for food.

17 To say something. Contains smaller word peak.

18 Thick fat or oil.

20 A compound work — break + fast.

21 A nut the size of a pea. A compound word.

22 A piece of meat. Homophone for stake.

23 Not able to hear.

Down

2 Something that is worth a lot of money. Rhymes with measure.

3 Part of your body. Rhymes with bread.

4 To have plenty of money. Rhymes with healthy.

7 This person can teach.

8 A time when it is quiet or still. Homophone for piece.

9 Very, very good. Rhymes with mate.

11 To make someone happy. Rhymes with tease.

14 We do this to food. Rhymes with feet.

15 To damage something. Rhymes with rake.

16 Costs less than usual. Homophone for cheep.

19 A weed found in the sea. A compound word.

Note: It is important that words in mazes are written in the correct order from left to right and from the top to the bottom — not from right to left or from the bottom to the top. The importance of modelling conventional spelling cannot be overstated. Talk with the students about how knowing about spelling patterns will assist them when writing.

Crosswords and word mazes of this type help to focus on the visual image of the word. It is also useful to create crosswords where the clues for the crossword contain the same spelling pattern as the answer. For example:

A garden tool, same spelling pattern as cake. (rake)

Close by, same spelling pattern as heart. (near)

3 Build words around a spelling pattern

There are many words that can be formed by combining letters, prefixes and suffixes with a spelling pattern. For example, the students could combine the following letters and suffixes to form many *eigh* words.

w		t_____y
h		less _____ ness
fr	*eigh*	en
sl		ing
n		ed
		bor _____ ly

The students could then confirm their spelling attempts in a dictionary or wordbook. The words could then be regrouped according to the sound represented by the spelling pattern *eigh*. Ask them to think about how knowing about spelling patterns will assist them with their writing.

4 Building words

This game can be played in pairs and requires players to create words by combining letters and suffixes with a spelling pattern.

Example Spelling pattern *eigh*
When learning about the spelling pattern *eigh* the following words might be listed on the class list.

height	weight	neighbor	sleight	heighten
weights	weighty	neighborly	freight	freighting
freighted	weighted	neighboring	eight	eighteen
eightieth	eighty	heights	neigh	neighing
neighed	neighs	sleigh	sleighs	sleighed

These words from the class list could then form the basis of a game of word building. Each word from the list is written on a card. The letters or prefix before the spelling pattern are cut away and the letters or suffix after the spelling pattern are cut off. Consequently the word is cut into two or three sections. For example:

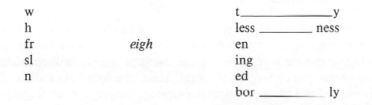

Word	Section 1	Section 2 (Spelling pattern)	Section 3
eightieth		eigh	tieth
		(word cut into two sections)	
sleigh	sl	eigh	
	(word cut into two sections)		
neighbor	n	eigh	bor
		(word cut into three sections)	

The word parts are then placed face down in three piles — one for each section of the word. The first pile of cards contains the letters or prefixes that occur at the beginning of the words, the second pile contains cards with the spelling pattern written on them and the third pile contains cards with the letters and suffixes that occur after the spelling pattern in the word. Players take turns in selecting a card from each pile. If the cards form a word the player writes it down and confirms the spelling in a dictionary, wordbook or on a class chart. If a word is not formed the cards are returned to their piles. After a limited period the player with the most words wins.

This game may be varied by cutting words into more than three sections, for example the word *neighborly* could be cut into four sections — n + eigh + bor + ly. Talk with the students about how learning about a spelling pattern will assist them with their writing.

5 Board games

Board games such as *Snakes and Ladders* may be adapted so that the players create words by combining letters, prefixes and suffixes with a spelling pattern.

The players throw a dice and move around the board. When they land on a square with a letter, prefix or suffix they combine it with the spelling pattern and write the word formed.

If players land on a snake they move down, if they land on a ladder they move up.

The player who has written the greatest number of words is the winner. Talk with the students about how learning about a spelling pattern will assist them with their writing.

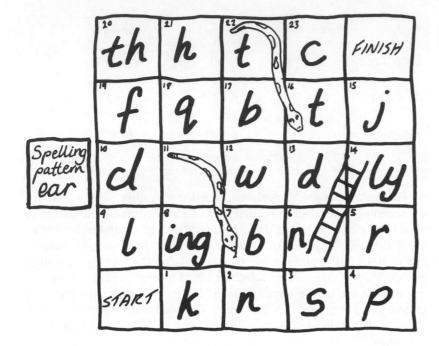

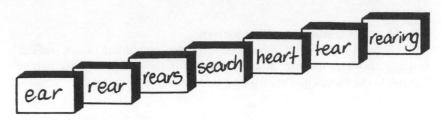

6 Card games

Card games such as *Dominoes, Concentration* and *Word Rummy* can be adapted to focus on a spelling pattern. Write the words with a common spelling pattern on small cards — one word on each card. Students can play these card games in pairs.

When playing *Dominoes* all cards are placed face down. The first player chooses a card and then chooses another. The word on the second card must begin with the last letter of the previous word, for example, *earth* then *heart*. If not it is placed face down again. The second player then chooses a card and then another. Again, the word on the second card must begin with the last letter of the previous word. The player who has the greater number of words in a line in a given time is the winner.

If players get stuck they may look in a dictionary or wordbook for other words with the common spelling pattern, or they may like to rearrange their words. Talk with the students about how learning about a spelling pattern will assist them with their writing.

When playing *Concentration* two sets of cards are required. The sets of cards are mixed and placed face down and each player takes turns in turning up two cards. If the cards are the same the player keeps them. If not, they are placed face down again. The game continues until all pairs are matched and the player with the greater number of matching cards is the winner. Talk with the students about how learning about a spelling pattern will assist them with their writing.

Word Rummy may be played in pairs or small groups. Players create words by combining letters, word parts and suffixes with a spelling pattern. Use a class list of words with a common spelling pattern, for example *augh*.

caught	daughter	slaughter	laughter	draught
laugh	taught	draughty	laughed	haughty
naughty	laughing			

Take words from the class list and make card sets of letters, for example *c, d, dr, l, h, ty* and so on, and suffixes, for example *er, ing*, and so on, found in the words on the class list. Make multiple cards with the spelling pattern *augh*.

Each player is given a set of approximately ten spelling pattern (*augh*) cards. Five cards (word parts and suffixes only) are then dealt out to each player and the excess cards placed face down in a stack.

Players use cards in their own hands to combine with spelling pattern cards (*augh*) to form words. For each turn the player draws a card (word part or suffix) from the stack, forms a word if possible and discards one card (word part or suffix). Players have the option of picking up a card from the discard pile rather than drawing from the face down pile. Players write down words formed and confirm them against the class list. The player with the greatest number of words in a given time wins. Talk with the students about how learning about a spelling pattern will assist them with their writing.

7 Build words from a short word
This activity focuses on the possible letter sequences in the English written language.

Start with a common word, such as *an* and build words by adding a letter at a time. Note that the sequence of letters is not altered. For example:

an   and   sand   stand

Alternately, choose a word from which new words may be made by deleting a letter. For example:

there   here   her   he

Looking closely at words develops a writer's visual memory of such words. Encourage the students to look for the smaller words within a word, such as *an* and *he* in the examples above. Talk with the students about how looking for smaller words within words often assists writers to attempt to spell unknown words.

8 Words within words
This activity involves students in finding smaller words within words, without changing the sequences of letters. This helps students see the visual patterns within words and develops their visual memory of such words.

Looking for smaller words within words also assists writers to spell unknown words. For example, if wanting to spell the word *mother* some students may see smaller words within it they can already spell (*moth*, *other*, *her*, *the*, *he* or *her*). Thus when they attempt to write the word *mother* they know it should contain the word or words they can already spell.

Show the students how to set out their work — by writing the smaller words directly below their position in the original word. For example:

```
knowledgeable
know
   owl
      ledge
           able
now
      edge
      led
no
```

To assist the students lines could be drawn to indicate the number of smaller words within the word. For example:

knowledgeable

———

——

——

——

——

——

This task could be made more difficult by simply indicating the number of words within the word, for example, *knowledgeable* (eight). Ask the students to think about how this will help them when writing.

9 Hangman
This activity focuses on the possible letter sequences in the English written language. Play *Hangman* as usual but encourage the students to make guesses based on the possible letter sequences rather than guessing wildly.

c – – – –

Talk with the students so that they realize the only letters that could follow the *c* would be *a, e, h, i, l, o, r, u, y* or *z*.

c h – – –

Continue to talk with students about the possibilities that now exist.

c h i – –

In order to encourage this logical guessing, play this game as a class before students play it in pairs. Ask the students to think about how this will help them when writing.

10 Word blanks

To encourage the knowledge of sequential probability of letters, provide the first and last letters of a word, with students listing as many words as possible by inserting a given number of letters. For example:

p – – d

paid, pond, prod, plod.

If played in pairs, the one who writes the most words in any given time is the winner. Ask the students to think about how this will help them when writing.

11 Letter mix-up

This activity focuses on the serial probability of letters in the English written language. Players play this game in pairs or small groups using a set of letters (with multiples of each letter and more of the more frequently used letters). Score one point for each letter used.

Place all letters face down. Each player selects eight letters and attempts to make a word. Players total their score after each word. Letters may then be rearranged or used with new letters to form new words. If letters can be rearranged players score double points:

m e a t   m a t e   t e a m   t a m e

m a t e s

Ask the students to think about how this will help them when writing.

12 Word pyramids

This activity focuses on the serial probability of letters in the English written language. Develop word pyramids by increasing either the number of letters or syllables each time:

at
rat
rate
crate
crater

cab
cabin
cabinet

any
anyhow
anybody

This activity may be varied by starting with the word at the bottom of the pyramid and students deleting a letter or syllable each time. Talk with the students about how adding or deleting a letter often changes the pronunciation of a word and how knowing this will assist them when writing.

13 Manipulating words

This activity focuses on the serial probability of letters in the English written language. Write as many words as you can think of, the letters of which may be:

- reversed to form a new word, e.g. spot/tops
- reversed to form the same word (palindromes), e.g. madam
- changed in sequence to form a new word (anagram), e.g. dare, read, dear.

Ask the students to think about how knowing this will help them with their writing.

14 Word chains

This activity focuses on the serial probability of letters in the English written language. A word chain is formed when one letter is changed in a word to form another word and this continues in a number of steps. The word chains can have various levels of difficulty. For example:

cold – co_d – _ord – w_rd – warm

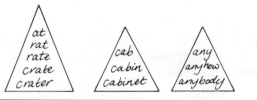

lost – ____ – ____ – home

Encourage students not to have wild guesses but to think about the possible letter sequences. They may use a dictionary or wordbook to assist them. Encourage them to think of different ways of completing word chains. Ask them to think about how this will assist them when writing.

Resources

Alphabet Wall Frieze, Usborne.
Base, Graeme, *Animalia*, Viking Kestrel.
Beck, Ian, *Little Miss Muffet*, Oxford. (Predicting words with the first few letters as a clue.)
Blake, Quentin, *Quentin Blake's ABC*, Collins Picture Lions.
Brown, Mic, *ABC*, Kingfisher Books.
Crane, Walter, *An Alphabet of Old Friends*, Thames and Hudson.
Crossword Magic, L & S Computerware, Mindscape.
Dahl, Roald, *The BFG*, Puffin. (Common spelling patterns used to make new words.)
Hughes, Shirley, *Lucy and Tom's a.b.c.*, Little Picture Puffin.
James, Ann, *One Day: a Very First Dictionary*, Oxford.
King, Clive, *The Twenty-two Letters*, Puffin.
Kipling, Rudyard, 'How the First Letter was Written' and 'How the Alphabet Began' in *Just So Stories*.
Lionni, Les, *The Alphabet Tree*.
Martin, Bill Jr., & Archenbill, *Chick a boom*, Scholastic, USA.
McNaughton, Colin, *ABC and Things*, Macmillan.
Milne, A.A., *Winnie the Pooh ABC Frieze*, Methuen.
Pelham, David, *A is for Animals*, Macmillan.
Rowe, Jeanette, *The At Home Alphabet Frieze*, Oxford.
Scarry, Richard, *Find Your ABC*, Collins Picture Lions.
Snowball, Diane, & Green, Robyn, *My Picture Dictionary*, Oxford.
Super Wordfind, Hartley Courseware, Dataflow.
Van Allsburg, Chris, *The Z was Zapped*, Houghton Mifflin.

Common sounds

Although the English written language uses an alphabet of 26 letters (graphemes) there are 44 distinctive sounds (phonemes) in English oral language. To inform students that a letter has only one sound is incorrect; the sound associated with a particular letter is dependent upon the word in which it occurs. A common sound is a sound that is common to a number of words. A variety of letters or spelling patterns may represent a common sound.

It is interesting to note that there is some discussion about which letters represent a particular sound. For example, in a word such as *write*, we consider that the letters *wr* represent the /r/ sound, that *w* is not a silent letter; while others consider the letter *r* represents the /r/ sound and the *w* is silent.

Below is a list of common sounds. This list is provided as a resource of the range of common sounds and the varieties of ways they may be represented. It is not intended as a list of words to be learned. Note that the words listed may not be in the appropriate grouping if they are pronounced differently in your country or region. Even within your own classroom you may find the students pronounce the same words differently, each pronunciation being acceptable.

/a/	as in clap	/u/	as in mud	/o/	as in shop
a	pat	u	pup	o	top
ai	plait	o	front	oh	Johnson
i	meringue	oe	does	ho	honor
al	salmon	ou	touch	a	was
ua	guarantee	oo	blood	ow	knowledge
		a	above	ou	cough
				au	because
				e	entree

/i/	as in knit	/e/	as in get	/er/	as in mother
i	pit	e	pet	or	doctor
ie	sieve	ie	friend	er	bother
u	busy	ea	dead	yr	martyr
o	women	ai	said		
y	syrup	u	bury		
e	pretty	a	any		
ui	build	ue	guess		
		ei	leisure		
		eo	leopard		

/ay/	as in play		/ie/	as in pie		/oh/	as in Joh
a	acorn		i	sigh		o	photo
ay	day		y	type		oe	hoe
ey	prey		i	find		ow	yellow
eigh	weigh		igh	light		owe	owes
aigh	straight		ie	lie		oa	loaf
ei	reindeer		eye	eyes		oh	oh
ai	train		eigh	height		ew	sew
ea	great		is	island		eau	beau
et	bouquet		ais	aisle		ough	though
au	gauge		ig	sign		au	chauvinist
e	debut		a	naive		ot	depot
ee	matinee		ai	Shanghai		oo	brooch
aig	campaign		ui	guide		ol	folk
						ou	cantaloupe

/ee/	as in knee		/ar/	as in car		/or/	as in for
e	these		a	last		aw	paw
i	ski		ar	garden		augh	taught
ee	feet		aar	bazaar		our	four
ei	ceiling		ear	heart		or	for
ie	believe		au	aunt		ore	more
ea	tea		er	sergeant		oor	floor
eo	people		ah	galah		au	because
oe	amoeba		al	half		oar	board
ay	quay		are	are		al	talk
is	chassis		uar	guard		a	all
es	chasses		at	nougat		ure	sure
ey	key					ar	wharf
ae	archaeology					ort	rapport
						aur	dinosaur
						orp	corp
						orps	corps

/ooh/	as in pooh		/ere/	as in there		/yoo/	as in youth
o	who		ere	where		u	education
oo	room		eir	their		eau	beauty
wo	two		are	mare		eu	Europe
oe	shoe		air	pair		ewe	ewe
ough	through		ayor	mayor		u	use
ou	group		ear	bear			
ue	true						
u	Honolulu						
ui	fruit						
ew	jewel						
ut	debut						
hou	silhouette						

/ow/	as in now		/ir/	as in fir		/ere/	as in here
ow	cow		ear	earth		ere	mere
hou	hour		ir	thirty		ear	fear
ou	house		er	fern		eer	beer
ough	bough		ur	turn		eir	weird
			or	world		eor	theory
			olo	colonel			

/oo/	as in book		/oy/	as in boy
oo	look		oi	oil
oul	would		oy	toy
u	push		uoy	buoy
			oig	poignant

/t/	as in to		/z/	as in doze		/s/	as in sing
t	top		s	is		s	us
tt	little		ss	possess		ss	assist
te	late		se	nose		se	promise
ed	finished		si	business		c	conceit
cht	yacht		es	clothes		ce	lace
ct	indict		x	xylophone		sw	sword
pt	receipt		z	zebra		st	listen
tte	cigarette		zz	buzz		sc	scythe
th	thyme					ps	psalm
bt	doubt					sth	asthma

/m/	as in mud	/n/	as in in	/f/	as in father
m	me	n	on	f	if
mm	common	nn	inn	ff	off
me	time	ne	lane	fe	life
mb	comb	kn	know	ph	photograph
gm	diaphragm	dne	Wednesday	lf	half
mn	hymn	pn	pneumonia	gh	trough
lm	calm	gn	gnat	u	lieutenant
				ft	soften

/d/	as in dog	/w/	as in wet	/j/	as in jug
d	said	w	will	j	joke
dd	muddy	wh	when	g	giant
de	made	o	once	d	soldier
ed	rolled	ul	suite	dge	judge
ld	would	u	language	ge	cage

/p/	as in peg	/b/	as in bin	/g/	as in go
p	pet	b	bit	g	give
pp	pepper	bb	rubber	gg	trigger
pe	pipe	be	robe	gh	ghost
				gue	vague

/k/	as in king	/sh/	as in shop	/r/	as in rabbit
k	kite	sh	fish	r	rat
kk	trekked	t	nation	rr	terror
ke	like	s	sugar	re	more
ck	duck	ce	ocean	rre	bizarre
ch	chorus	ss	tissue	wr	write
c	cat	sc	conscience	rh	rhythm
che	ache	sch	schedule	rt	mortgage
lk	talk	ch	chalet	rrh	diarrhoea
qu	quay	chs	fuchsia		
que	antique				
kh	gymkhana				

/l/	as in log	/th/	as in this	/h/	as in hug
l	let	th	then	h	he
ll	yellow	the	bathe	wh	who
le	hole				

/kw/	as in quick	/x/	as in fox	/y/	as in yellow
qu	queen	xe	axe	y	yacht
ch	choir	x	mix	i	Australia
cu	cuisine	cks	bricks		
		cc	accept		

/ch/	as in chip	/v/	as in very	/ng/	as in sing
ch	chicken	v	every	ng	wrong
te	righteous	f	of		
c	cello				
t	creature	schwa/a/	as in ago		
tch	witch	schwa/e/	as in taken		
cc	cappuccino	schwa/i/	as in pencil		
cz	Czech	schwa/o/	as in lemon		
		schwa/u/	as in circus		
		schwa/ia/	as in marriage		

Points to think about

Points to consider when students are learning about common sounds include:

▼ *Introducing common sounds*

There is no point in dealing with common sounds until students show in their writing that they are trying to represent sounds they hear. They also need to know the names of the letters to have the language to talk about which letters represent particular sounds.

▼ *Listening for a common sound*

It is important to give students clear, consistent instructions and to ensure they understand that they *listen* for a common sound in a word. Initially it may be fun to wear some big ears to cue students into listening for a sound. In this way they will not confuse *listening* for common sounds with *looking* for letters or spelling patterns.

Initially, when students are listening for a common sound it may help if they do not see the words, and they concentrate on listening. This eliminates the possibility of students confusing the /**ee**/ sound with the letter *e* they might see in a word such as *egg*.

▼ *Thinking about the letter or spelling patterns that represent a common sound*

It is vital in a spelling program to develop class word lists and to draw attention to them for writing. Class spelling lists should be developed to focus on a common sound. By listing words with a particular sound and noting the symbols that represent that sound and the positions in which various letters or spelling patterns occur in a word students begin to realize:

* that a sound may be represented by a variety of spelling patterns or letters
* the position in which a sound occurs in a word will often influence the choice of letter or letters. For example, the common /**f**/ sound may be represented by the letters *f*, *ff*, *ph*, *gh*, *lf* and *ft*. However, if the /**f**/ sound is at the beginning of the word it will only be represented by the letter

f or the spelling pattern *ph*. If it is at the end of the word it is not likely to be represented by *ft*, for example, in the words *off*, *cough*, *graph*, *if*, *half*, *puff*, *laugh*, and *tough*. Where the spelling pattern *ft* is at the end of the word it is not likely to represent the /**f**/ sound, for example, *soft*, *lift*, *left* and *craft*.

▼ *Assisting inexperienced writers to identify sounds in words*

Assist students to understand that sounds heard in a word provide an indication of the way a written word may be represented. The following techniques used by Elkonin (1973) may be necessary:

* A student is given pictures of objects. Below each picture is a rectangle divided into squares according to the number of sounds, not letters, in the name of the object.
* The student is then given some counters. The teacher slowly articulates each word and then the student says the word aloud, and places a counter for each sound heard in the corresponding square of the diagram below the picture.

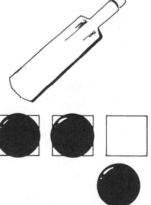

* This activity is gradually changed from an oral analysis with the use of counters and squares to a silent activity. Once the writer can identify the sounds and their order, the concept that letters represent sounds may be introduced.

  This procedure has also been used by Marie Clay.

▼ *Assisting inexperienced writers to identify letters that represent sounds*

When inexperienced writers are attempting to write an unknown word encourage them to listen to the sounds they hear in it. Assist them by asking the questions:

What do you hear first?
What do you hear next . . .?
What do you hear last?

Once students have identified a sound in the word assist them to find a letter that represents the sound, using an alphabet strip. Move along the strip from left to right saying the names of the letters. When you reach the letter that represents the sound assist the students to identify the letter and encourage them to write the letter.

For easy reference place an alphabet strip on the table in front of each student. Encourage clear pronunciation and articulation of words.

▼ *The importance of clear articulation*

Provide a correct model of pronunciation and encourage students to articulate words clearly. Observe students who seem to be having speech problems, but remember that it may be developmental. If necessary seek specialist assistance.

When students are attempting to spell an unknown word, as well as using the letter-name strategy (*lft* for *elephant*, *ne* for *any*) they use the position of articulation of a letter to assist them identify and write the necessary letter. Consequently, because some letters are articulated in precisely the same way you will find students substituting such letters on that basis.

For example, the following letters are articulated in the same position and are commonly substituted by inexperienced writers:

e for *i* — *es* (is)
a for *e* — *wat* (went)
g for *k* — *drg* (drink)
d for *t* — *doy* (toy) etc.

It is important to appreciate that students using the position of articulation when selecting letters to write do not have a 'vowel problem' and are not confusing the sounds. It is just that they are also taking into account the position of articulation of the sound made.

▼ *Teaching common sounds and letters or spelling patterns exclusively of each other*

If focusing on a common sound and a letter or spelling pattern in the one week try to keep them exclusive of each other until the students fully understand that they *listen* for a common sound and *look* for letters or spelling patterns. For example, if listening for the /e/ sound do not study a letter or spelling pattern that is related to the sound /e/, such as *ea* or *e*.

▼ *Teaching blends is not helpful*

When attempting to spell an unknown word inexperienced writers *analyze* a word into its component sounds, and attempt to identify the letters that represent those sounds. Consequently, teaching students blends does not provide them with a useful strategy for writing. It is also worth noting that blending, or synthesizing sounds in a word is a more difficult task than analyzing a word into its sound components.

▼ *Teaching about common sounds that are relevant to students' writing needs*

There is no particular sequence in which common sounds should be studied. Those occurring in many words students are reading at that time and require for their personal writing needs are the common sounds that should be dealt with at any given time. It may be that a common sound is studied on more than one occasion in a particular year level, and it may be that the same common sound is also studied again in subsequent years, depending on the writing needs of the students. If a common sound is studied on more than one occasion it is likely that the words being studied will be different words.

▼ *Thinking about the terms long and short vowel*

Instead of using the terms *long* and *short vowel* which may be confusing to some less experienced writers, it is only necessary to refer to the different sounds, such as /ee/ or /e/. You could also refer to the sound that is the same as the letter name (rather than long vowel) or not the name of the letter (rather than short vowel). Students are familiar with and understand the term *letter name*. For example, if students are focusing on the /ee/ sound it is easy for them to understand that it is the same as the name of the letter *e*.

There is also no need to refer to a long or short vowel when referring to the sounds in a word. For example, the sounds are:

/**a**/ as in c**a**t or /**ay**/ as in d**ay** or pl**a**te
/**e**/ as in br**ea**d or /**ee**/ as in k**ey** or m**e**
/**i**/ as in p**i**g or /**ie**/ as in s**igh** or b**uy**
/**o**/ as in s**a**lt or /**oh**/ as in b**oa**t or kn**ow**
/**u**/ as in m**o**ther or /**yoo**/ as in **you**th or be**au**ty.

As students become experienced writers it is more relevant to use the terms *long* and *short vowel*.

▼ *Pronunciation*

It is important to talk with the students about the way a word is pronounced since this will affect the way it is grouped. For example, in the word *again* the letters *ai* may be pronounced as /**ay**/ or /**e**/. If the letters are pronounced as /**ay**/ then the word would appear on the /**ay**/ list. If pronounced as /**e**/ the word would appear on the common sound /**e**/ list and not on the /**ay**/ list. Discuss with the students how some words are pronounced differently in different English speaking countries and even in the same country there are different dialects or variations in pronunciation.

▼ *Forming a generalization about the letters* i *and* e *together*

When students are learning about the /ee/ sound it would be an appropriate time to assist them to form a generalization about when the letter *i* comes before the letter *e* and when the letter *e* comes before the letter *i*. To assist students to notice when this occurs, the words from the /ee/ class list

containing the spelling patterns *ie* or *ei* could be listed separately to specifically highlight when the letter *i* comes before *e*, and when the letter *e* comes before *i*. For example:

bel**ie**f	rece**i**pt
th**ie**f	c**ei**ling
f**ie**ld	rece**i**ve
n**ie**ce	dec**ei**ve
p**ie**ce	s**ei**ze

Encourage the students to write the generalizations in their own words, and use the following statement as a guide to what you might discuss with them and lead them to understand.

If *i* and *e* together have the sound of *e*, the *i* comes first except after *c*. For example:

field	receive
grief	ceiling
niece	receipt
piece	

Exceptions: seize	seizure

Talk with them about how after the letter *c* the spelling pattern *ei* is consistent, and that it also occurs in the word *seize* and other words in the *seize* word family, such as *seizure* and *seized*. Assist the students to review and refine their generalizations as they discover other words with *i* and *e* together in their reading and writing.

Activities

These activities can be used to help students learn about common sounds:

▼ *Listening for rhyming words*

Involve the students in rhyming activities.
* Identify and list rhyming words in a song or poem and underline the rhyming parts of each word. Note whether they have the same or different

letters or spelling patterns. List other words which rhyme with the listed words. For example:

> Little Jack **Horner**
> Sat in the **corner**
> Eating his Christmas **pie**
> He put in his **thumb**
> And pulled out a **plum**
> And said what a good boy am **I**.

List other words which rhyme with the listed words and note whether they have the same or different spelling patterns:

> **Horner, corner,** sauna . . .
> **thumb, plum,** come, chum, some . . .
> **pie, I,** eye, high, buy, tie, try . . .

- Ask students to suggest words which rhyme with a particular word, such as *take* — break, fake, ache, cake, lake.
- Listen for words which rhyme: bad, run, none, happy, fun.

▼ *Playing rhyming games*

Rhyming Ping-Pong

Students play in pairs. The object is to name as many rhyming words as possible within a given time. The player who calls out the last word when the time runs out is the winner. For example, the first player says *stay*, second player says *weigh*, and so on. This game could be played with the entire class, perhaps in relay. The teacher could list the words and the list could then be used to discuss the rhyming parts of each word and note whether they have the same or different letters or spelling patterns.

Hocus Pocus

Play in pairs with students naming two rhyming phrases within a given time, for example, *night-flight, golden-holden, money-honey* and *great-mate*. The player who calls out the last rhyming phrase when the time runs out is the winner. If possible write these phrases on cards so that the students can underline the rhyming parts of each word and note whether they have the same or different letters or spelling patterns.

▼ *Developing class lists*

Class lists could be developed as students discover that a sound may be represented by a letter or variety of spelling patterns. Start separate class lists for some of the common sounds students have encountered and encourage the students to add words that they find in their personal writing or reading to the appropriate lists. Ask the students to underline the common sound in each word and talk with them about the letter or various spelling patterns that represent each sound. Ask them to think about how this will help them when they are writing. For example:

> We listened for the /u/ sound in these words. Which letters represent the /u/ sound?
> love cousin mother brother cut alone country touch blood flood flooded does front pup doesn't hug run jump young upon once one won stung uncle above among
>
> We regrouped the words according to the spelling pattern that represented the /u/ sound.
>
> | love | above | cut | young | does | blood |
> | mother | alone | pup | cousin | doesn't | flood |
> | brother | among | hug | country | | flooded |
> | one | | run | touch | | |
> | once | | jump | | | |
> | won | | upon | | | |
> | front | | uncle | | | |
> | | | stung | | | |

*Year 1 students listened for /u/ words when being read to. The /u/ words were listed then regrouped according to the letter or spelling pattern that represented the /u/ sound. Note: Some words could be placed in two groups — **above** and **among**.*

When focusing on a common sound the students may be asked to listen to a story, poem, instructions, and so on, with the purpose of listening for words which contain a particular sound. They could also search their personal writing, class charts, topic lists and reading materials. As students identify words that contain the common sound these could also be added to the class charts, and the letter or spelling patterns that represent the common sound identified.

It is important to remember when studying a common sound, that all words the students suggest that contain the sound, regardless of the letters that represent that sound, should be listed. Here is an example procedure for exploring any common sound:

If students are asked to listen for the /ay/ sound then words such as *explain*, *spray*, *great*, *weigh*, *reindeer*, *grey*, *fete* and *reign* should be accepted if the students know the meanings of such words.

A class spelling list could then be developed that focuses on the common sound /ay/.

It may contain words similar to the following:

spr<u>ai</u>n	creche	sl<u>eigh</u>	pl<u>ay</u>	del<u>ay</u>	sail
gr<u>ey</u>	break	crepe	entr<u>ee</u>	gr<u>ea</u>t	sale
st<u>ea</u>k	fr<u>a</u>me	tr<u>ay</u>	l<u>a</u>te	gr<u>a</u>de	tail
ag<u>ai</u>n	w<u>eigh</u>t	matin<u>ee</u>	camp<u>aig</u>n	fete	pr<u>ey</u>

The students could then be asked to say each word aloud and to listen for the common sound and identify its position in the word. The spelling pattern or letter that represents the common sound could then be underlined.

Explain to the students that the common sound /ay/ is represented by a variety of letters and spelling patterns. Ask the students to group the /ay/ words from the list above so that those with the same letter or spelling pattern are together. For example:

pl<u>ay</u>	creche	entr<u>ee</u>	gr<u>ea</u>t	camp<u>aig</u>n	pr<u>ey</u>	w<u>eigh</u>t	l<u>a</u>te
tr<u>ay</u>	crepe						
del<u>ay</u>	fete						

Ask them to think about which is the most common letter or spelling pattern that represents the /ay/ sound and also discuss the positions in the words of the letter and various spelling patterns. For example:

Does the letter *e* ever represent the /**ay**/ sound at the beginning of a word?
Does the letter *e* ever represent the /**ay**/ sound at the end of a word?
Does the letter *e* ever represent the /**ay**/ sound in the middle of a word?

Add to the class charts as students find more /**ay**/ words in reading materials, their personal writing and in the classroom. When listing words with a common sound ensure the students understand their meanings and that they are words they are likely to use in their writing.

Repeat this procedure with other common sounds relevant to students' writing needs. Ask the students to think about how knowing about common sounds and the letters or variety of spelling patterns that represent these will assist them with their writing.

▼ Publishing a big book

When the students have listed a reasonable number of common sounds assist them to publish a big book of sounds. This could consist of the collated class charts or it may be a separate publication. Involve the students in deciding on the organization of the book. A contents page could be included for easy reference. Students may also like to include a page on which they each write something that they have learned about common sounds. The big book could be placed in the class library for the students to refer to or borrow.

Contents

Sounds we listen for:

	Page
/u/ sound	2 - 3
/u/ sound sorted into groups - different letters represent the /u/ sound - ou, o, u, oe, oo.	4 - 8
/sh/ sound	9 - 10
/sh/ sound sorted into groups - different letters represent the /sh/ sound - cc, ch, sh, t, s, c, ss.	10 - 16
/m/ sound	
/m/ sound sorted into groups - different letters represent the /m/ sound - m, mb, mm	17 - 18

The contents page from Year 1's big book of common sounds.

▼ *Students complete activities with common sounds*

It may become apparent during discussions with students or from reading their writing that further clarification of their understandings about common sounds is necessary. If this is so, students could complete activities similar to the following and could also create such activities for their peers to complete. The words selected for the activities should be taken from class lists, students' writing and reading materials, lists of words they have selected to learn, topic lists, and other sources that are relevant to them.

1 Listening for sounds

Ask the students to listen for a particular sound in the initial and final positions of words. For example:

- What sound can you hear at the beginning of these words: sausage, snake, sun?
- Clap when you hear the /**b**/ sound at the beginning of a word: cap, bad, tomato, ball.
- Which words have /**d**/ at the end: bad, yellow, mad, dad, jump?

2 Listening for alliteration

- Alliteration is the occurrence of the same letter or sound at the beginning of several words in succession. Help students recognize the repeated sound in an alliterative text, for example the /**p**/ sound in *Peter Piper picked a peck of pickled peppers* and the /**k**/ sound in *Crazy koalas kiss crocodiles and chemists at Christmas*. Write the sentences that contain alliteration on class charts and highlight the repeated sound and the letter or spelling patterns that represent the repeated sound.

Crazy koalas kiss croaking crocodiles and chemists at Christmas.

- Read books where alliteration is used as a literary device, for example, *Grandma Goes Shopping, Animalia, Pride of Lions, The Z was Zapped* and *The King Who Sneezed* (see Resources, page 66). Place these books in the class library for the students to take home and read with their parents. The students may like to make their own book of alliterative sentences.

3 Tongue twisters

This activity focuses on tongue twisters that often use alliteration. For example:

> She sells sea-shells on the sea-shore.
> The shells she sells are sea-shells, I'm sure,
> For if she sells sea-shells on the sea-shore,
> Then I'm sure she sells sea-shore shells.

Read the students some tongue twisters from *Faint Frogs Feeling Feverish* (see Resources, page 66). Identify the repeated sound or sounds, for example /s/ and /sh/ in the example above, and underline the letter or spelling pattern that represents the repeated sounds. Use a different color to underline each letter or spelling pattern. Make a class book of tongue twisters. Allow time for the students to learn a tongue twister and present it to the class and encourage the students to write their own tongue twisters. Their presentations could be taped.

4 Limericks

This activity focuses on tongue twisters that sometimes appear in the form of limericks. For example:

> A flea and a fly in a flue
> Were imprisoned, so what could they do?
> Said the fly, 'Let us flee,'
> Said the flea, 'Let us fly,'
> So they flew through a flaw in the flue.

> There was an old man from Peru
> Who dreamed he was eating his shoe.
> He woke in a fright
> In the middle of the night
> And found it was perfectly true.

Read the students some limericks from *Loads and Loads of Limericks* (see Resources). Identify the repeated sound or sounds in each limerick, for example /f/ and /ooh/ in the first example above, and the /ooh/ sound in the second example. Underline the letter or spelling pattern that represents the repeated sounds. Use different colors to underline each letter or spelling pattern. Make class books of limericks and place them in the library for the students to borrow. Allow time for the students to learn some limericks to present to the class. Their presentations could be taped.

5 Spoonerisms

A spoonerism occurs when letters in two or more words are changed unintentionally, for example, 'When the team lost it was a blushing crow' — instead of 'crushing blow'. Read *Spooner or Later* (see Resources) to the students and as other spoonerisms occur when students are talking discuss them. The students may like to develop a class list of spoonerisms. It may be of interest to the students to know that the word spoonerism was named after W. A. Spooner, a reverend famous for making slips when talking.

6 Substituting letters

Choose a word that students know and substitute letters to form new words. Ask the students how one word may be changed to form the next one and how knowing this will assist them with their writing.

pop	pot	p**o**t
dot	po**d**	pi**t**
rot	**po**p	p**e**t
not	. . .	. . .
. . .		

Develop the list as the students suggest the substitution of a letter. Do not present students with the list of words.

▼ *Homophones*

A homophone is one of a set of words (two or more) that sound the same but are spelled differently because they have different meanings, such as *their*, *there*, and *they're*. It is important to teach students the meaning of each homophone so that they know which of the set to use in their writing.

Talk with the students about the words *stair* and *stare* and the different spelling patterns that represent the same sound, such as *air* and *are* representing the /**air**/ sound respectively.

Resources

Armitage, Ronda and David, *Grandma Goes Shopping*, Picture Puffin. (Alliteration.)

Base, Graeme, *Animalia*, Viking Kestrel. (Alliteration.)

Harris, David, G., *Loads and Loads of Limericks*, Angus & Robertson.

Huth, Angela, *Island of the Children*, Orchard Books. (Contains poems about words.)

Jennings, Paul, Greenwood, Ted, & Denton, Terry, *Spooner or Later*, Viking. (Spoonerisms.)

McGough, Roger, *Nailing the Shadow*, Viking Kestrel. (Contains poems full of word play.)

Morgan, Nicola, *Pride of Lions*, Fitzhenry & Whiteside, Ontario. (Alliteration, homographs and homonyms.)

Reeves, James, *Ragged Robin: Poems from A to Z*, Walker Books. (Alliteration, a poem for each letter of the alphabet.)

Obligado, Lilian, *Faint Frogs Feeling Feverish*, Picture Puffin. (Tongue twisters.)

Van Ahlsberg, Chris, *The Z was Zapped*, Houghton Mifflin. (Alliteration.)

McAllister, Angela, *The King Who Sneezed*, Aurum Books for Children. (Alliteration.)

Homophones

Homophones are words (two or more) that sound the same but have different meanings and are spelled differently.

Below is a list of common homophones. This list is provided as a resource of the range of homophones and it is not intended as a list of words to be learned.

ail ale	*air heir*
aisle I'll isle	*allowed aloud*
altar alter	*ark arc*
aren't aunt	*ate eight*

bail bale

ball bawl

fair fare

farther father

bare bear

barren baron

fate fete

feat feet

bass base

beach beech

fiancé fiancée

find fined

bean been

beat beet

fir fur

flare flair

berry bury

berth birth

flea flee

flew flue flu

bite bight

blew blue

floor flaw

flour flower

bore boar

bored board

for fore four

foreword forward

border boarder

bolder boulder

fort fought

forth fourth

bough bow

boy buoy

fowl foul

frank franc

brake break

bread bred

freeze frieze

bridle bridal

buy bye by

caddie caddy

cygnet signet

gait gate

gamble gambol

caste cast

canvas canvass

gaol jail

genes jeans

caught court

caster castor

gild guild

gilt guilt

cellar seller

cell sell

gnaw nor

gnu new knew

cereal serial

cent scent sent

gorilla guerrilla

grate great

cheap cheep

chased chaste

grease Greece

grill grille

chews choose

cheque check Czech

groan grown

guessed guest

chute shoot

choral coral

coarse course

cite site sight

hail hale

hair hare

complement compliment

colonel kernel

hall haul

hanger hangar

conker conquer

cord chord

hart heart

hay hey

core corps

council counsel

heal heel he'll

hear here

creak creek

currant current

heard herd

heed he'd

hew hue

high hi

days daze

dear deer

him hymn

hire higher

desert dessert

dew due Jew

hoard horde

hoarse horse

die dye

died dyed

hole whole

holy wholly

do dew due (U.S.A.)

doe dough

hour our

draft draught

draw drawer

duel dual jewel

dying dyeing

I aye eye

idle idol

in inn

island Ireland

earn urn

eaves eve

its it's

except accept

eye I

kerb curb

key quay

knead need

knight night

knot not

know no

knows nose

lane lain
law lore
leak leek
lei lay
liar lyre
load lode
lock loch

larva lava
lead led
leant lent
lesson lessen
licence license
loan lone
loot lute

maid made
main mane
mantel mantle
meet meat
metal mettle
mind mined
miner minor
moan mown
morn mourn

mail male
manner manor
mare mayor
meddle medal
meter metre
might mite
missed mist
moor more
muscle mussel

nave knave
none nun

net nett
nit knit

oar ore or awe
one won

oh owe

pail pale
pair pear pare
pastel pastille
pause paws pores pours
peace piece
pedal peddle
pistol pistil
plain plane
poll pole
pray prey
pride pried
profit prophet

pane pain
passed past
patience patients
paw poor pour pore
peel peal
peer pier
place plaice
plum plumb
practice practise
prays praise
principal principle
prise prize

quarts quartz

queue cue

racket racquet
raise rays
raw roar
real reel
read reed
ring wring
roe row
root route

rung wrung
rain reign rein
rapped rapt wraped
read red
right rite write
road rode rowed
role roll
rose rows

sale sail
saw soar sore
sealing ceiling
seas sees seize
sense cents
sew sow so
shear sheer
shore sure
sight site cite
sleight slight
source sauce
stare stair
steak stake
stile style
sun son
sundae Sunday

scull skull
seam seem
seen scene
serf surf
sewn sown
shoe shoo
side sighed
slay sleigh
some sum
stalk stork
stationary stationery
steal steel
storey story
straight strait
suite sweet

tail tale
taught taut
tear tier
tern turn
theirs there's
throne thrown
tire tyre

tare tear
tea tee
teem team
their there they're
threw through
tide tied
to too two

toe tow	*tor tore*
towed toad	*troop troupe*
urn earn	
vain vein vane	*vale veil*
wail whale	*waist waste*
wait weight	*waive wave*
war wore	*ware wear*
warn worn	*watt what*
way weigh	*we wee*
weak week	*we're wear where*
wears where's	*weather whether wether*
weave we've	*we'd weed*
weigh whey	*weighed wade*
were whirr	*which witch*
whine wine	*who's whose*
wood would	*wrote rote*
yolk yoke	*yore you're your*
you ewe	

Points to think about

Points to consider when students are learning about homophones include:

▼   *Homophones, homographs and homonyms*

Talk with the students about the differences between homophones, homographs and homonyms.

Homophones are words (two or more) that sound the same but have different meanings and are spelled differently. Explain to the students that the word homophone is formed from the two derivatives *homo* (same) and *phone* (sound).

Homographs are words that are spelled the same way but are pronounced differently and have different meanings, for example, *minute* (element of time) and *minute* (small). Explain to the students that the word homograph is formed from the two derivatives *homo* (same) and *graph* (writing).

Homonyms are words that are spelled the same way and sound the same but have different meanings, for example, *bat* (an animal) and *bat* (used to hit a cricket ball).

▼   *Introducing homophones*

Once students have a body of words they recognize and are able to identify words that sound the same, it is appropriate to introduce homophones.

▼   *Pronunciation*

It is important to talk with the students about the way a word is pronounced since this will determine if words are homophones or not. For example, the word *buoy* in America is pronounced as *boo-ey*, and *dew* and *due* would be homophones for *do*.

Discuss with the students how some words are pronounced differently in different English speaking countries and even in the same country there are different dialects or variations in pronunciation.

▼   *The spelling of a homophone depends upon its context — its meaning*

It is important to teach students the meanings of each homophone in a set so that they know which of the set to use in their writing, since the conventional spelling of a homophone depends upon its context. It is significant that when teaching spelling this is the only time it is necessary for students to write the words being studied in sentences, since the spelling of a homophone is determined by its context.

Otherwise, class lists which highlight the relationships that exist between words and the types of activities suggested in this book are of greater benefit in assisting students to learn about the relationships between words in the English written language than is the writing of unrelated words in sentences. This is the difference between spelling activities and vocabulary activities. Spelling activities highlight the various relationships between words in order to provide writers with strategies when they are attempting unknown words in their writing. However, vocabulary activities do not teach writers these strategies, but require them to focus on the meanings of words.

▼ *Homophones have common sounds represented by different spelling patterns*

Talk with the students about the different spelling patterns that represent the same sound, for example the spelling patterns *ower* and *our* represent the **/our/** sound in the homophones fl**ower** and fl**our**.

▼ *Confirming the spelling of homophones*

Encourage the use of a dictionary or wordbook to confirm the spelling of homophones.

▼ *Teaching about homophones that are relevant to students' writing needs*

There is no particular sequence in which homophones should be studied. Those students require for their personal writing needs are the homophones that should be dealt with at any given time. It may be that a homophone is studied on more than one occasion in a particular year level, and it may be that the same homophone is also studied again in subsequent years, depending on the writing needs of the students.

Activities

The following activities can be used to help students learn about homophones:

▼ *Developing a class list*

As the students discover homophones when reading or when they begin using them in their writing start a class list of homophones and encourage the students to add to the list as they find others. When listing homophones ensure the students understand their meanings and that they are words they are likely to use in their writing. It would be useful to include illustrations or sentences that indicate the meanings of each homophone. Encourage students to refer to resources such as *The Australian Writer's Wordbook* to check homophone meanings.

Ask the students to think about how knowing about homophones will help them when attempting to spell unknown words in their writing.

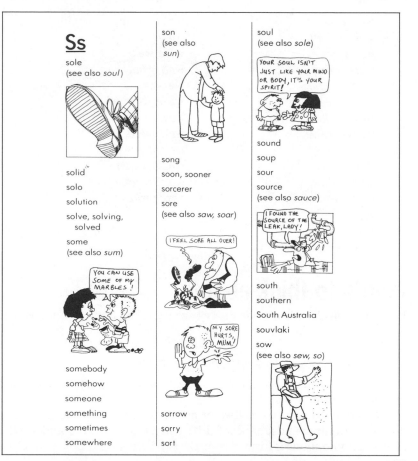

A page from The Australian Writer's Wordbook *in which the meaning of homophones is conveyed in the artwork.*

▼ *Publishing a big book*

When the students have listed a reasonable number of homophones assist them to publish a big book. This could consist of the collated class charts or it may be a separate publication where one set of homophones is featured on each page. Involve the students in deciding on the organization of the book. A contents page could be included for easy reference. Students may also like to include a page on which they each write something that they have learned about homophones. The big book could be placed in the class library for the students to refer to or borrow.

A group of Year 6 students prepared a page for their class big book of homophones after reading the books A King Who Reigned *and* A Chocolate Moose for Dinner.

▼ *Using literature as a model for students' writing*

Read the books *A Chocolate Moose for Dinner* and *The King Who Reigned* (see Resources, page 72) to the students. These humorous books contain many homophones and provide students with models for writing similar homophone books.

A Year 6 student published this poster about the homophones **pail** *and* **pale**.

▼ *Students complete activities with homophones*

It may become apparent during discussions with students or from reading their writing that further clarification of their understandings about homophones is necessary. If this is so, students could complete activities similar to the following and could also create such activities for their peers to complete. The words selected for the activities should be taken from class lists, students' writing and reading materials, lists of words they have selected to learn, topic lists, and other sources that are relevant to them.

1   Memory aids and homophones

Assist the students to form memory aids related to homophones. For example:

> I h**ear** with my **ear**.
> I'll stay h**ere**, you go over t**here**.
> **Their** — indicates possession; an **heir** will inherit and gain possession of something.
> A set of **tw**ins is **tw**o children.
> The w**itch** has an **itch**.
> The princi**pal** is your **pal**.
> Pract**ice** is a noun; **ice** is a noun.
> Pract**ise** is a verb; **is** is a verb.

It may be necessary for students to use a wordbook such as *The Australian Writer's Wordbook* to assist them. Ask the students to think about how memory aids will help them with their spelling.

2   Playing games with homophones

To further clarify students' understandings about homophones select some of the games in Chapter 11 to play, using homophones. The homophones selected for the activities should be taken from class lists, students' writing and reading materials, lists of words they have selected to learn, topic lists, and other sources that are relevant to them.

Resources

Gwynne, Fred, *The King Who Reigned*, Prentice-Hall, New York, 1970.
Gwynne, Fred, *A Chocolate Moose for Dinner*, Prentice-Hall, New York, 1976.
Snowball, Diane and Morrish, Gwen, *The Australian Writer's Wordbook*, Nelson, Melbourne, 1984.

The Structure of Words

6

Derivatives

A derivative is a word part that has come from another language. Many derivatives have come from Latin and Greek, and some have also come from Old French.

Below is a list of common derivatives. This list is provided as a resource of the range of derivatives and it is not intended as a list of words to be learned.

L = Latin   Gk = Greek   OF = Old French

Derivative	Meaning	Example	Origin
acouo	*I hear*	*acoustics*	*Gk*
acro	*furthest point, summit*	*acrophobia*	*Gk*
aequi	*equal*	*equity*	*L*
aero	*air*	*aerodrome*	*Gk*
agogue, gogy	*leader*	*pedagogue*	*Gk*
agri	*field*	*agriculture*	*Gk*
akrobatos	*walking up high*	*acrobat*	*Gk*
allelos	*another*	*allelomorphic*	*Gk*
alter	*other*	*alternate*	*L*
alti, altus	*high*	*altitude*	*L*
ambi	*both*	*ambidextrous*	*L*

Derivative	Meaning	Example	Origin
amphi	*both*	*amphitheatre/ amphitheater*	*Gk*
una	*against*	*anachronism*	*Gk*
annus	*year*	*annual*	*L*
anonymos	*without name*	*anonymous*	*Gk*
ante	*before*	*antenatal*	*L*
anth	*flower*	*polyanthus*	*Gk*
anthrop	*man, human being*	*anthropology*	*Gk*
aqua	*water*	*aquatics*	*Gk,L*
arachno	*spider*	*arachnology*	*L*
urbor	*tree*	*arboriculture*	*L*
arch, archeo	*ruler, chief*	*monarch, architect*	*Gk*
archaeos	*old, primitive*	*archaeology/ archeology*	*Gk*
arthron	*joint*	*arthritis*	*Gk*
assembler	*to gather*	*assemble*	*OF*
aster, astron	*star*	*astrology*	*Gk*
athlon	*contest*	*pentathlon*	*Gk*
atmosphaera	*vapor spheres*	*atmosphere*	*L*
audio	*to hear*	*auditorium*	*L*
auris	*ear*	*aural*	*L*
aurum	*gold*	*aurous*	*L*
auto	*self*	*autocrat*	*Gk*
avis	*bird*	*aviary*	*L*

Derivative	Meaning	Example	Origin
bakterion	*small stick*	*bacterial*	*L*
baculus	*rod, staff*	*bacillus*	*L*
baros	*weight, heavy*	*barometer*	*Gk*
batos	*walking*	*acrobat*	*Gk*
belli	*war*	*belligerent*	*L*
bene	*well*	*benevolent*	*L*
bi, bin	*two*	*bicycle*	*L*
biblio	*book*	*bibliography*	*Gk*
bios	*life*	*biology*	*Gk*
botanicus	*herbs*	*botany*	*Gk*
brachio	*arm*	*Brachiosaurus*	*L*
bronchi	*windpipe*	*bronchitis*	*L*
cali, calli	*beauty*	*calligraphy*	*Gk*
carni	*flesh*	*carnivorous*	*L*
capio, captum	*take*	*capture*	*L*
cardia, cardio	*heart*	*cardiac*	*Gk*
carto, charto	*map*	*cartographer*	*Gk*
cedo, cessum	*I go, yield*	*proceed, concede*	*L*
centum	*a hundred*	*century*	*L*
cephal	*head*	*encephalitis*	*Gk*
cheiria, chiria	*type of hand*	*chiropractic*	*Gk*
chloro	*light green*	*chlorine*	*Gk*
chroma, chromatis	*color*	*chromatic*	*Gk*
chronos	*time*	*chronology*	*Gk*
chryso	*gold*	*chrysanthemum*	*Gk*
cidal, cide	*slayer*	*homicidal*	*L*
cine	*ashes*	*incinerator*	*L*
cine	*motion, moving*	*cinema*	*L*
citare	*to witness*	*cite*	*L*
civis	*citizen*	*civics*	*L*
claustro	*an enclosure*	*claustrophobia*	*L*
clude	*shut*	*conclude*	*L*
conflictus	*strike together*	*conflict*	*L*
corpus	*body*	*corpse*	*L*
cosmo	*tidy, ordered*	*cosmetic*	*Gk*
cosmo	*of the world*	*cosmopolitan*	*Gk*

Derivative	Meaning	Example	Origin
costa	*rib, flank*	*coast*	*L*
cotyl	*cup shaped*	*dicotyledon*	*Gk*
cracy, crat	*power*	*democrat*	*Gk*
crania, cranial	*skull*	*cranium*	*Gk*
cryo	*icy cold*	*cryogenics*	*Gk*
crypto	*hide*	*cryptic*	*Gk*
curro, cursum	*run*	*current*	*L*
cuspis	*point*	*cusp*	*L*
cyclos	*wheel*	*bicycle*	*Gk*
cyclos	*circle, circular*	*cyclone*	*L*
cytos	*cell*	*phagocyte*	*Gk*
dactyl	*fingers, toes*	*pterodactyl*	*Gk*
deca	*ten*	*decade*	*Gk*
deci	*a tenth of*	*decimal*	*L*
dei, deo	*of a god*	*deity*	*L*
demi	*a half*	*demigod*	*OF*
demos	*the people*	*democracy*	*Gk*
dendro	*tree*	*rhododendron*	*Gk*
dens, dentis	*tooth*	*dentist*	*L*
derma, dermatos	*skin*	*dermatitis*	*Gk*
dexio, dextra	*the right hand*	*dextrous*	*L*
dico, dictum	*speak*	*dictate*	*L*
dies	*day*	*diurnal*	*L*
doxy	*opinion*	*orthodoxy*	*Gk*
duplo	*doubling*	*duplicate*	*L*
dys	*bad, badly*	*dysentery*	*Gk*
eid, eido	*image*	*kaleidoscope*	*Gk*
elasto	*flexible*	*elastic*	*Gk*
electro	*beaming sun*	*electricity*	*Gk*
embryo	*swelling within*	*embryo*	*Gk*
equus	*horse*	*equestrian*	*L*
ergon	*work*	*ergonomic*	*Gk*
ethnos	*race, nation*	*ethnology*	*Gk*
ethos	*behavior*	*ethical*	*Gk*

Derivative	Meaning	Example	Origin
eu	*well*	*euphoria*	*Gk*
exo	*outside*	*exodus*	*Gk*
facilis	*easy*	*facilitate*	*L*
facio	*face*	*facial*	*L*
factum	*make, do*	*factory*	*L*
ferri, ferro	*iron*	*ferro-magnetic*	*L*
fero, ferens	*bear, carry*	*transfer*	*L*
ferrum	*iron*	*ferro-alloy*	*L*
finis	*end*	*final*	*L*
flori	*flower*	*florist*	*L*
formis	*shaped*	*uniform*	*L*
fortis	*strong*	*fortress*	*L*
frater	*brother*	*fraternity*	*L*
frigus	*cold, coldness*	*refrigeration*	*L*
fugio, fugitum	*flee*	*fugitive*	*L*
gage	*pledge*	*mortgage*	*L*
galactia, galacto	*milk*	*galaxy (Milky Way)*	*Gk*
gaster, gastros	*belly*	*gastronomy*	*Gk*
ge, geo	*earth*	*geography*	*Gk*
genero, generatum	*produce*	*generate*	*L*
gero, geri	*old age*	*geriatric*	*Gk*
gingivo	*gums*	*gingivitis*	*L*
glaci	*ice*	*glacier*	*L*
gnosis	*to know*	*prognosis*	*Gk*
gonia	*angle, corner*	*octagon*	*Gk*
grade, gradio	*step, stepping*	*retrograde*	*L*
gram, gramo	*letters of the alphabet*	*telegram*	*Gk*
grapho	*I write*	*autograph*	*Gk*
gratia	*favor*	*ingratiate*	*L*
gravis	*heavy*	*gravity*	*L*
gyne, gynaecos	*woman*	*gynaecology/ gynecology*	*Gk*
gyro	*circular*	*gyrocopter*	*Gk*

Derivative	Meaning	Example	Origin
haema	*blood*	*haemorrhage/ hemorrhage*	*Gk*
hekaton	*a hundred*	*hectare*	*Gk*
heli	*to roll*	*helicopter*	*Gk*
helios	*the sun*	*heliograph*	*Gk*
hemi	*half*	*hemisphere*	*Gk*
hepat, hepato	*liver*	*hepatitis*	*Gk*
hept	*seven*	*heptagon*	*Gk*
herbi	*grass*	*herbivore*	*L*
heteros	*other*	*heterosexual*	*Gk*
hexa	*six*	*hexagon*	*Gk*
hieros	*holy*	*hierarchy*	*Gk*
hippos	*horse*	*hippodrome*	*Gk*
homeosis	*like, similar*	*homograph*	*Gk*
horo	*hour*	*horoscope*	*Gk*
horti	*garden*	*horticulture*	*Gk*
hydro	*water*	*hydroponics*	*Gk*
hypno	*sleep*	*hypnosis*	*Gk*
iatros	*healing*	*psychiatry*	*Gk*
idem	*same*	*identical*	*L*
ideo	*language, thought*	*ideology*	*Gk*
idio	*one's own, private*	*idiosyncrasy*	*Gk*
igneo, igni	*fiery, burning*	*igneous*	*L*
inferus	*lower, beneath*	*infernal*	*L*
infestus	*hostile*	*infection*	*L*
innovare	*renew, start again*	*innovate*	*L*
ject	*throw, cast*	*projected*	*L*
juris	*law*	*jurisdiction*	*L*
juxta	*nearby*	*juxtapose*	*L*
khiton	*coat of mail*	*chiton*	*Gk*
khloros	*green*	*chlorophyll*	*Gk*
khoreia	*a dance*	*choreography*	*Gk*
kilo	*one thousand*	*kilogram*	*Gk*

Derivative	Meaning	Example	Origin
kinesi	*movement*	*kinesthetic*	*Gk*
klept, klepto	*thief*	*kleptomaniac*	*Gk*
labio	*lips*	*labium*	*Gk*
lacti, lacto	*milk*	*lactate*	*L*
lamina	*thin sheet, layer*	*laminex*	*L*
lati	*wide, broad*	*latitude*	*L*
lecto	*pick, select*	*collect*	*Gk*
leuco	*white*	*leucocyte*	*Gk*
lepsia, lepsis	*seizure*	*epilepsy*	*Gk*
lexis	*speech*	*dyslexic*	*Gk*
lexico	*vocabulary*	*lexicon*	*Gk*
liber	*free*	*liberalize*	*L*
lingua	*the tongue*	*linguist*	*L*
lipo	*fats*	*lipid*	*Gk*
lithos	*stone*	*monolith*	*Gk*
littera	*letter*	*alliteration*	*L*
loger, logy	*speech, thought*	*logic*	*Gk*
locus	*place*	*allocate*	*L*
loquence, loquy	*speaking*	*soliloquy*	*L*
lucidus	*light giver*	*lucid*	*L*
lumen	*light*	*luminous*	*L*
luni	*moon*	*lunacy*	*L*
lusis, lysis	*freeing, dissolving*	*analysis*	*Gk*
macros	*large, long*	*macrobiotic*	*Gk*
magnus	*large*	*magnitude*	*L*
male	*bad, badly*	*malefactor*	*L*
mammi	*breast*	*mammogram*	*L*
mania	*madness*	*maniac*	*Gk*
manus	*hand*	*manuscript*	*L*
marinus	*of the sea*	*maritime*	*L*
mater, matris	*mother*	*matriarch*	*L*
medius	*middle*	*Mediterranean*	*L*
mega, megalos	*large*	*megaphone*	*Gk*
melo	*song*	*melodrama*	*Gk*
menti	*of the mind*	*mental*	*L*

Derivative	Meaning	Example	Origin
mensis	*month*	*semester*	*L*
mesos	*middle*	*Mesopotamia*	*Gk*
meter, metros	*mother*	*metropolis*	*Gk*
metron	*measure*	*meter*	*Gk*
mille	*one thousand*	*millipede*	*Gk*
mimo	*mimic*	*mimicry*	*Gk*
minimus	*smallest*	*minimal*	*L*
misos	*hatred*	*misogynist*	*Gk*
mitto, missum	*send*	*missile*	*L*
mnesis	*memory, remembering*	*amnesia*	*Gk*
moles	*a mass*	*molecule*	*L*
monos	*one*	*monopoly*	*Gk*
moros	*stupid, foolish*	*sophomore*	*Gk*
morphe	*form*	*amorphous*	*Gk*
mortis	*dead*	*mortgage*	*L*
multus, multi	*many, much*	*multitude*	*L*
murus	*wall*	*mural*	*L*
museo	*museum*	*museology*	*Gk*
myein	*to shut*	*myopia*	*Gk*
myelia, myelitis	*marrow, spinal chord*	*osteomyelitis*	*Gk*
mykes	*mushroom*	*mycobacteria*	*Gk*
natus	*birth*	*natal*	*L*
navilis	*ship*	*navy*	*L*
nekros	*corpse*	*necropolis*	*Gk*
neos	*new*	*neolithic*	*Gk*
neuron	*nerve*	*neurology*	*Gk*
nomen	*name*	*nominate*	*L*
nihil	*nothing*	*annihilate*	*L*
nomos	*system of laws*	*astronomy*	*Gk*
nostos	*return home*	*nostalgia*	*Gk*
novem	*nine*	*November*	*L*
novus	*new*	*novel*	*L*
nox, noctis	*night*	*nocturnal*	*L*
nullis	*nothing, none*	*nullify*	*L*

Derivative	Meaning	Example	Origin
nuncio	speak out	announce	L
nutri	nourish	nutritious	L
octo	eight	octopus	Gk,L
oculus	eye	oculist	L
hodos	pathway	odometer	Gk
odon, odus	tooth	orthodontist	Gk
oecos	house, environment	ecology	Gk
omnis	all	omnipotence	L
onym	name	synonym	Gk
ophthalmos	eye	ophthalmologist	Gk
opia	eye	myopia	Gk
opticus	sight	optical	Gk
orama	sight, view, spectacle	diorama	Gk
orexia	appetite, strong desire	anorexia	Gk
ori	mouth, of the mouth	orifice	L
ornithos	bird	ornithology	Gk
orthos	straight, normal	orthography	Gk
osteo	bone	osteometry	Gk
paidos	of a child	pediatrics/ paediatrics	Gk
palaeos	old	palaeontology	Gk
parens	parent	parenting	L
pars, partis	part	compartment	L
pathos	suffering	sympathy	Gk
patior, patiens	suffer	patient	L
patri	father	patriarch	Gk
pedi	foot	pedicure	L
pello, pellens	drive, push	repel	L
penta	five	pentagon	Gk
pepsia	digestion	dyspepsia	Gk
phago	I eat	phagocyte	Gk

Derivative	Meaning	Example	Origin
pharmaco	drug, medicine	pharmacist	Gk
pheno	appear	phenomenon	Gk
philo	loving, fond of	bibliophile	Gk
phobos	fear of	phobia	Gk
phono	sound, voice	telephone	Gk
phoro	bring, carry	semaphore	Gk
phos, photos	light	photograph	Gk
phyllon	leaf	chlorophyll	Gk
plagiarus	kidnapper	plagiarize	L
plebi	people (excluding nobility)	plebeian	L
plegia	a stroke, blow	quadriplegic	Gk
plex, plicate	to fold	complicated	L
pluris	more, several, many	plural	L
pneumo	air, breathe	pneumonia	Gk
pod, podous	foot	podium	Gk
poeia	poetry	onomatopoeia	Gk
polio	grey (matter of brain)	poliomyelitis	Gk
polis	city	metropolis	Gk
politikos	civic, political	political	Gk
ponere	place	hydroponics	L
portare	carry	portable	L
positus	placed	position	L
postero	behind	posterior	L
potamus	river	hippopotamus	Gk
praxis, practic	performance of movements	chiropractic	Gk
primi, primo	first	primary	L
prudentia	knowledge	prudent	Gk
pseudo	false	pseudonym	Gk
psyche	the mind	psychology	Gk
ptero	winged, feathers	pterodactyl	Gk
pulmo	lungs, belly	pulmonary	L
puter	rotten	putrefy	L

Derivative	Meaning	Example	Origin
pyo	pus	pyorrhoea	Gk
pyr	fire	pyromaniac	Gk
qualis	of what type	quality	L
quantus	of what amount	quantity	L
quattuor	four	quadrangle	L
quinque	five	quinquennial	L
quintus	fifth	quintet	L
radius	radiant energy	radium surgery	L
rect	ruled straight	rectangle	L
regi	king	regent	L
renis	kidney	renal	L
rhodo	rose	rhododendron	Gk
rogo	I ask	interrogation	L
rota	wheel	rotate	L
rrhage	bursting forth	hemorrhage/haemorrhage	Gk
rrhoea	to flow	diarrhoea	Gk
sacer, sacrum	holy	sacred	L
sali	salt	saline	L
sancti	holy	sanctify	L
sangui	blood	sanguine	L
sani	healthy	sanitation	L
saurus	lizard	dinosaur	Gk
schizo	split	schizophrenia	Gk
scope	to regard, view	stethoscope	Gk
sect, sected	to cut	bisect	L
scribe	write	transcribe	L
seismos	to shake, earthquake	seismology	Gk
sema	signal, sign	semaphore	L
semi	half	semicircle	L
sepsis	putrification of body part	septic	Gk

Derivative	Meaning	Example	Origin
septem	seven	September	L
servo	keep	conserve	L
sex	six	sextuplet	L
skelos	leg	isosceles	Gk
sol	sun	solar	L
solari	to comfort	console	L
soli	alone, solely	soliloquy	L
solvo, solutum	solve, solution	dissolve	L
sonans, soni	sound producing	resonance, sonic	L
sopor	deep sleep	soporific	L
sophia	wisdom	philosopher	Gk
spasmos	spasm	spasmodic	Gk
spectro	look	inspect	L
sphero	sphere	atmosphere	Gk
spiro	breathing	respiration	L
statatus	set up, standing	status	L
stella	star	constellation	L
steno, stenosis	close, little	stenographer	Gk
stereos	hard, solid	stereotype	Gk
stetho	chest, breast	stethoscope	Gk
sthenos	strength	callisthenics	Gk
stipare	press together	constipation	L
strati	spread out, a covering	strata	L
strophe	a turning	catastrophe	Gk
structus	built	construction	L
sui	of oneself, of one's own	suicide	L
sympho	harmonious	symphony	Gk
synchro	simultaneous	synchronize	Gk
tactus	touch	tactile	L
tauto	the same	tautology	Gk
taxis	an arrangement	taxonomy	Gk
techni	art, skill	technique	Gk
tecton	a builder	architect	Gk
tele	from a distance	telephone	Gk

Derivative	Meaning	Example	Origin
tensus	*stretch*	*tensile*	*Gk*
terra	*earth*	*terrain*	*L*
tertia	*third*	*tertiary*	*L*
theos	*god*	*theology*	*Gk*
therapaeia	*healing*	*therapy*	*Gk*
thermo	*hot*	*thermostat*	*Gk*
thrombo	*clot*	*thrombosis*	*Gk*
toma, tome	*cut*	*hysterectomy*	*Gk*
tonus	*sound*	*baritone*	*L*
topos	*position, place*	*isotope*	*Gk*
totus	*whole*	*total*	*L*
tractus	*drawn towards*	*attract*	*L*
trophia, tropho	*nutrition*	*dystrophy*	*Gk*
tropos	*to turn*	*tropics*	*Gk*
ty	*ten*	*twenty*	*OE*
ultra	*beyond*	*ultraviolet*	*L*
umus	*one*	*unit*	*L*
vale, valence	*be well, strong*	*equivalence*	*ML*
vari, vario	*both*	*variety*	*L*
veloci	*speed*	*velocity*	*ML*
venio	*come*	*convener*	*L*
ventri	*of the belly*	*ventriloquist*	*L*
video	*see*	*provide*	*L*
vita	*live*	*vital*	*L*
visere	*scrutinize*	*revision*	*L*
vitreo	*become glass like*	*vitrify*	*L*
vivi	*to be alive*	*revive*	*ML*
vocare	*to call*	*revoke*	*L*
voci	*voice*	*vociferous*	*L*
vora, vore	*eating*	*carnivore*	*ML*
vulni	*a wound*	*vulnerable*	*L*
zelous	*zeal*	*jealous*	*Gk*
zoon, zoa	*living thing*	*zoologist*	*Gk*

Points to think about

Points to consider when students are learning about derivatives include:

▼ *Introducing derivatives*

Once students have a body of words they recognize and they are starting to think about the meaning relationships between words, or are capable of thinking about these relationships, it is appropriate to introduce derivatives. It is also important to consider the development of students' oral vocabulary to ensure they understand the meanings of many words which contain a particular derivative.

▼ *Knowing about the spelling of a derivative gives writers power when using the English written language*

Explain to the students that each derivative has a particular meaning and is usually spelled the same way. Ensure the students understand that if they know how to spell a derivative in one word, for example, *chloro* in *chlorophyll* it will help them to spell it in other words, for example, *chlorine* and *chlorinate*.

▼ *The position of derivatives in words*

A derivative may occur in various positions in a word, for example *photo* in the words **photo**graph and tele**photo**, but the spelling is still the same.

▼ *Teaching about derivatives that are relevant to students' writing needs*

There is no particular sequence in which derivatives should be studied nor should all derivatives be studied. It is more important that students understand that derivatives form part of the basic organizational structure of words in the English language and that such knowledge can help their spelling.

The derivatives students require for their personal writing needs are those that should be dealt with at any given time. It may be that a derivative is studied on more than one occasion in a particular year level, and it may be that the same derivative is also studied again in subsequent years, depending on the writing needs of the students. If a derivative is studied on more than one occasion it is likely that the words being considered will be different words.

Activities

The following activities can be used to help students learn about derivatives:

▼ *Developing a class list*

As the students discover derivatives when reading or when they begin using them in their writing start a class list of words with derivatives and encourage students to add to the list as they find others. When listing words with derivatives ensure the students understand their meanings and that they are words they are likely to use in their writing. Ask the students to underline the derivative in each word and talk with them about what a derivative is, ensuring that they understand it is a word part that has come from another language, for example Latin, Greek, and Old French.

Using words from the class list explain to the students that a derivative is always spelled the same way and always has the same meaning. Ask them to think about how this will help them when attempting to spell unknown words in their writing.

▼ *Classifying derivatives*

As the class list of derivatives develops assist the students to classify the words according to their derivatives, for example, all words with the derivative *thermo* or *phono* would be grouped together. Start a class chart for each derivative and encourage the students to add words with the derivative that they find in their personal writing or reading.

Choose one derivative to focus on, this being the one that will be most useful for the students to know about for their personal writing, for example *bene*. Ask students to search for words containing *bene*. Again, they could search their personal writing, class charts, topic lists and reading materials. Ask them to think about the meaning of the derivative *bene* and the way it is spelled consistently in each word. Repeat this procedure with other derivatives listed on the class list or those that occur in the students' writing.

▼ *Publishing a class book*

When the students have listed a reasonable number of derivatives help them publish a book. This could consist of the collated class charts or it may be a separate publication. Involve the students in deciding on the organization of the book, for example, the derivatives could be arranged alphabetically or according to their country of origin. A contents page could be included for easy reference. Students may also like to include a page on which they each write something that they have learned about derivatives. The book could be placed in the class library for the students to refer to or borrow.

Derivative	Country of Origin	Page
tele (from a distance)	Gk.	1-2
haema (blood)	Gk.	3
bene (well)	L	4
cardio (heart)	Gk	5
aqua (water)	Gk/L	6
marinus (sea)	L	7
scope (view)	Gk	8-9

The contents page from a big book of derivatives being studied in a Year 5 class.

▼ *Students selecting words to learn*

Some of the words students select to learn may contain derivatives, for example, *scope* in stetho**scope**. It is useful for them to find and list other words with the same derivative, for example, peri**scope**, tele**scope**, micro**scope**, and so on. Ask the students to think about how learning other words with the same derivative will help them with their writing.

▼ *Students complete activities with derivatives*

It may become apparent during discussions with students or from reading their writing that further clarification of their understandings about derivatives is necessary. If this is so, students could complete activities similar to the following and could also create such activities for their peers to complete. The words selected for the activities should be taken from class lists, students' writing and reading materials, lists of words they have selected to learn, topic lists, and other sources that are relevant to them.

Students can conduct a word search for words containing a particular derivative, for example, the derivative *cardio*. These are added to a class list or book. For example:

The derivative *cardio* means *heart*. Here are some words that contain the derivative *cardio*. Underline the part of the word that is based on the derivative *cardio*.

cardiac   cardiologist

Use your dictionary to find other words that contain the derivative *cardio* and note their meanings. Write the words with *cardio* that you think will be useful in your own writing.

....
....
....
....

Ask the students to think about how knowing about derivatives will help them with their writing.

Many games may be played using derivatives. Refer to Chapter 11.

Resources

Carroll, David, *The Dictionary of Foreign Terms in the English Language*, Hawthorn Books, New York, 1973.

Hall, Timothy, *How Things Start*, Collins, Sydney, 1979.

Morris, William and Mary, *Dictionary of Word and Phrase Origins*, Harper & Rowe, New York, 1962.

Pickles, Colin & Meynell, Laurence, *The Beginning of Words — How English Grew*, Anthony Blond, London, 1970.

Roget's Thesaurus of Words and Phrases (many publishers).

Shipley, Joseph T, *Dictionary of Word Origins*, Littlefield, Adams & Co., Iowa, 1957.

Prefixes

A prefix is a word *(under)* or word part *(un)* placed in front of a word to add to or change its meaning.

Below is a list of common prefixes. This list is provided as a resource of the range of prefixes and is not intended as a list of words to be learned.

a — not, without	*asymmetrical*
ab — away from	*abnormal*
ad — to stick to, against	*adhesive*
amphi — both, around	*amphibian*
ante — before	*antecedent*
anti — against, opposite	*anticlockwise*
arch — chief, senior	*archbishop*
at — to, toward	*attend*
auto — self	*autobiography*
bi — two, twice	*bicycle*
be — about, become	*befriend*
cata — down	*catastrophe*
circum — around	*circumnavigate*

co — together	co-operate
con — with, together	construct
contra — against	contradict
counter — in opposition, against	counteract
de — down, away from	dejected
deca — ten	decathlon
demi — half	demi-god
di — two	dicotyledon
dia — through, across	diameter
dis — not, do the opposite	discontinue
dys — bad, badly	dysfunction
en — to cause, provide	enable
endo — internal	endocrine gland
epi — to, against, added on	epigram
equi — equal	equilibrium
ethno — race, nation	ethnography
ex — out of, away from	exceed
ex — former	ex-wife
exo — outside	exoskeleton
extra — beyond, outside	extraordinary
fore — previously, in front of	forecast
hydro — water	hydro-electric
hyper — extra, over, beyond	hypercritical
hypo — under, below	hypodermic
il — not	illegal
im — not	impossible
in — within, into	include
in — not	inhuman
infra — below, underneath	infrastructure
inter — among, between	interstate
intra — inside	intramuscular

intro — inwards	introvert
ir — not	irreligious
iso — equal	isobar
macro — large	macrobiotic
mal — bad, wrongful	maltreat
meta — altered, behind	metamorphosis, metacarpal
micro — very small	microscope
mini — small	minibus
mis — wrongly, badly, not correct	misinform
mono — one, single	monopoly
multi — many	multimillionaire
necro — dead	necropolis
neo — new	neonatal
non — against, not	nonsense
ob — in the way of	obstruct
octa — eight	octagon
omni — all, general	omnipresent
pan — whole	panorama
par — equal	parity
para — alongside, similar to	paraphrase
patri — father	patriarch
per — through, thorough	perception
peri — around, about	perimeter
poly — many	polygon
post — after	postscript
pre — before	prejudge
pro — in favor of, forwards	proclaim, projectile
proto — earliest, original	prototype
pseudo — pretended, not real	pseudonym
quadri — four	quadrilateral

re — back, again	*reappear*
retro — backward	*retrospect*
self — of, over oneself	*self-control*
semi — half, partially	*semi-circle, semidetached*
step — relationship not due to blood, but remarriage	*stepfather*
sub — under, near, further	*submarine, subtropical, subcontract*
super — over, superiority, extra	*superstar*
supra — above, beyond	*supranational*
tetra — four	*tetralogy*
trans — across, beyond	*transaction, transcend*
tri — three	*triangle*
ultra — beyond	*apart*
un — not, the reverse of	*unaccompanied*
under — below, beneath	*underwear*
uni — single, one	*uniform*
up — up	*upwards*
via — by way of, through	*viaduct*
vice — in place of	*vice-captain*

Points to think about

Points to consider when students are learning about prefixes include:

▼ *Introducing prefixes*

Once students have a body of words they recognize and they are starting to think about the meaning relationships between words and the construction of words; or they are capable of thinking about these relationships, it is appropriate to introduce prefixes. It is also important to consider the development of students' oral vocabulary to ensure they understand the meanings of many words to which a prefix may be added

and the change in meaning as a result of a prefix being added, for example, the meaning of *happy* compared with *unhappy*.

▼ *Some prefixes change words to mean the opposite*

Some prefixes change words to mean the opposite of the base word. For example:

Base word	Prefix	New word
continue	dis	**dis**continue
logical	il	**il**logical
mature	im	**im**mature
numbered	un	**un**numbered
human	in	**in**human
reversible	ir	**ir**reversible

Talk with the students about possible reasons for the variety of prefixes meaning *not*, some of these being related to the ease of pronunciation of a word, for example the prefix *ir* before words that begin with *r* (regular/**ir**regular).

▼ *Many prefixes change words to have a different meaning*

Many prefixes change words to have a different meaning from the meaning of the base word. For example:

Base word	Prefix	New word
captain	vice	**vice**-captain
marine	sub	**sub**marine
action	trans	**trans**action
play	re	**re**play

▼ *Prefixes are always spelled the same way*

A prefix is always spelled the same way. If you know how to spell a prefix in one word it will help you spell it in other words. For example, if you can spell the prefix *pre* in *prefix* you can spell it in *preschool* and *prehistoric*.

▼ *Prefixes usually have the same meaning*

A prefix generally has the same meaning, for example, the prefix *mini* always means small. However, there are some prefixes that have more than one meaning, such as the prefix *ex* which means *out of* or *away from* and *former*.

▼ *Learning about what happens when you add a prefix that ends in the first letter of the base word*

When you add a prefix that ends in the first letter of the base word the newly formed word will have double letters. This is because a prefix is always spelled the same way and the base word also remains the same. For example:

un + natural = u**nn**atural
dis + satisfied = di**ss**atisfied
mis + spell = mi**ss**pell
im + mature = i**mm**ature
il + legal = i**ll**egal
ir + rational = i**rr**ational
un + necessary = u**nn**ecessary

Talk with the students about how knowing this will assist them when writing.

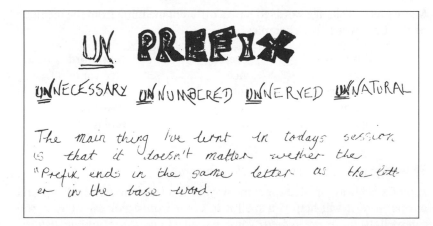

Adding prefixes.
When adding a prefix you always spell the base the word the same and the prefix the same. For example.

u̲n̲nescessary   You keep nescessary the same way. And also the prefix un. the same.

Two Year 5 students explain in their own words what happens when the prefix **un** *is added to words that begin with the letter* **n** *(below left, above).*

UN PREFIX

U̲N̲NECESSARY U̲N̲NUMBERED U̲N̲NERVED U̲N̲NATURAL

The main thing I've lernt in todays session is that it doesn't matter wether the "Prefix" ends in the same letter as the letter in the base word.

PREFIXE'S are not IRREGULAR.

irregular
irrelevent (ir rig levant)
irresistible
irreligious
irreconcilable
irrecoverable
irreducible
irrefutable
irregardless
irreplaceable
irrepressible

I know now how to use prefixes and if I use one like ir and add it to regular

ir + regular = irregular

But with dis+ appear = disappear.

just + the prefix don't change any-thing

A Year 5 student explains in his own words what happens when the prefix **ir** *is added to words beginning with* **r**.

▼ *Learning when to use hyphens when adding prefixes*

Prefixes do not generally require a hyphen. However, there are instances when they are used.

1 Hyphens are usually inserted when the last *vowel* of the prefix is the same as the first letter of the word to which it is being added. For example:

anti-intellectual   de-emphasise   pre-exist   re-elect

2 When a prefix *(re)* is added to a single-syllable word *(use)* and it results in two different vowels combining, a hyphen is inserted so that it does not read as a single syllable. For example:

re-use

3 If a word is in common usage the hyphen is sometimes omitted and the word written without a space. For example:

co-ordinate *or* coordinate   co-operate *or* cooperate

4 Where a prefix is being added to a word that consists of a base word plus suffix, and begins with a capital letter, a hyphen should always be inserted. For example:

un-Australian   anti-Semitism

5 The prefix *ex* means *out of, away from* (exceed) and *former* (ex-wife). When the prefix *ex* means *former* it is always followed by a hyphen.

6 A hyphen is also used to distinguish between base words with the same prefix. For example:

re-cover — to cover again, for example, a book
recover — regain, for example, strength
re-creation — to create again, renew
recreation — a restorative, relaxing pastime

▼ *Further clarifying the concept of a prefix*

Some words happen to begin with the same string of letters as a prefix, for example, *dis* in words like *discus* and *disperse, re* in *ready* and *reach,* and *pre* in *preach* and *precious*. Discuss such examples with the students.

▼ *Teaching about prefixes that are relevant to students' writing needs*

There is no particular sequence in which prefixes should be studied. Those students require for their personal writing needs are the prefixes that should be dealt with at any given time. It may be that a prefix is studied on more than one occasion in a particular year level, and the same prefix may also be studied again in subsequent years, depending on the writing needs of the students. If a prefix is studied on more than one occasion it is likely that the words being considered will be different words.

Activities

The following activities can be used to help students learn about prefixes:

▼ *Developing a class list*

As the students discover prefixes when reading or when they begin using them in their writing start a class list of words with prefixes and encourage them to add to the list as they find others. When listing words with prefixes ensure the students understand their meanings and that they are words they are likely to use in their writing. Ask the students to underline the prefix in each word and talk with them about what a prefix is, ensuring that they understand it is a word or word part placed in front of a word to add to or change its meaning.

Using words from the class list demonstrate to the students how the prefixes have been added to the base words by doing word sums similar to the following. For example:

Prefix	Base word	New word
re	+ play	= replay
un	+ happy	= unhappy

Ask the students to explain to each other the meanings of the new words formed with the prefixes plus the base words, for example, *replay*. Compare the meanings of these words with the original base words, in this example, *play*.

Explain to the students that a prefix is always spelled the same way and that the spelling of the base word does not alter when a prefix is added. Ask them to think about how this will help them when attempting to spell unknown words in their writing.

▼ *Classifying prefixes*

As the class list of prefixes develops assist the students to classify the words according to their prefixes, for example, all words beginning with the prefix *un* would be grouped together. Start a class chart for each prefix and encourage the students to add words that they find in their personal writing or reading to the lists.

Choose one prefix to focus on, this being the one that will be most useful for the students to know about for their personal writing, for example *dis*. Ask students to search for words containing *dis*. Again, they could search their personal writing, class charts, topic lists and reading materials. Ask them to think about the meaning of the prefix *dis* and the way it is spelled consistently in each word, and to observe the way the spelling of each base word does not change when the prefix *dis* is added.

Ask the students to explain what happens when a prefix, in this instance *dis*, is added to a base word that begins with the same letter, for example, *satisfied* — the newly formed word being *dissatisfied*. Continue to talk with them about how knowing about prefixes will assist them when they are attempting to spell unknown words in their writing. Repeat this procedure with other prefixes listed on the class list or which occur in the students' writing.

▼ *Publishing a book*

Assist the students to publish a book of prefixes. This could consist of the collated class charts or it may be a separate publication. Involve the students in deciding on the organization of the book. A contents page could be included for easy reference. Students may also like to include a page on which they each write something that they have learned about prefixes and how this will assist them with their writing. The big book could be placed in the class library for the students to refer to or borrow.

▼ *Students selecting words to learn*

Some of the words students select to learn may begin with a prefix, for example, *tricycle*, with the prefix *tri*. It is useful to list other words that contain the same prefix for students to learn, for example, *triangle, tripod, triplets* and to discuss with them why these other words have been listed. It is important that students understand that if they can spell a prefix in one word they can spell it in other words and that they therefore have a great deal of power when using the English written language.

▼ *Students searching for prefixes*

Students may conduct a word search for words containing a particular prefix, for example, *inter*. These words could then be added to a class list or book. During this activity some students may list words where the letters *inter* do not form a prefix, for example, in the word *interest*. When this occurs demonstrate to the students why the string of letters *inter* is not a prefix on this occasion, by separating the word in the following way — *inter + est*. In this way students can see that *est* is not a base word and therefore *inter* is not a prefix in the word *interest*. Also explain to them that the meaning of the prefix *inter* is not related in meaning to the word *interest*. Ask them to think about how this knowledge will assist them when they attempt to spell unknown words in their writing.

▼ *Students complete activities with prefixes*

It may become apparent during discussions with students or from reading their writing that further clarification of their understandings about prefixes is necessary. If this is so, students could complete activities similar to the following and could also create such activities for their peers to complete. The words selected for the activities should be taken from class lists, students' writing and reading materials, lists of words they have selected to learn, topic lists, and other sources that are relevant to them.

This activity focuses on the meaning and spelling of one prefix, for example, *re*. It highlights the way a prefix adds to or changes the meaning of a base word, and also demonstrates the consistent spellings and meanings of prefixes. For example:

Here are some words that contain the prefix *re*. Underline the prefix *re* in each word and complete the word sums. Then complete the statements about each *re* word.				

refill   =   re + ...   Refill means to ....
rename   =   .. + ...   Rename means to ....
re-enter   =   ... + ...   Re-enter means to ....
rewind   =   ... + ...   Rewind means to ....
rewrite   =   ... + ...   Rewrite means to ....
re-elect   =   ... + ...   Re-elect means to ....
reproduce =   ... + ...   Reproduce means to ....
rejoin   =   ... + ...   Rejoin means to ....

Write in your own words what happens when you join the prefix *re* to a word that begins with *e*.

Note: This activity also involves the students in thinking about the use of the hyphen when adding the prefix *re* to a word beginning with *e*.

It may become apparent during discussions with students or from reading their writing that further clarification of their understandings about prefixes is necessary. If this is so, students could play some of the games in Chapter 11 using prefixes. The words selected for the activities should be taken from class lists, students' writing and reading materials, lists of words they have selected to learn, topic lists, and other relevant sources.

Suffixes

A suffix is a letter or combination of letters added at the end of a word to form another word.

Below is a list of common suffixes. This list is provided as a resource of the range of suffixes and it is not intended as a list of words to be learned.

Suffixes that form nouns

▼ *Suffixes that often indicate a word is a noun*

— *ace*	*populace*
— *acity*	*tenacity*
— *al*	*removal*
— *ance*	*guidance*
— *ancy*	*occupancy*
— *ard*	*drunkard*
— *arian*	*vegetarian*
— *ence*	*independence*
— *ency*	*fluency*
— *ery*	*greenery*
— *ique*	*technique*
— *ization/isation*	*civilization/civilisation*
— *ment*	*advertisement*
— *ry*	*poetry*
— *ure*	*pleasure*

▼ *Suffixes to do with people*

1 Suffixes that indicate a person's occupation, position or activity

— *aire*	*millionaire*
— *ant*	*claimant*
— *ast*	*enthusiast*
— *ee*	*employee*
— *eer*	*engineer*
— *ent*	*student*
— *er*	*employer*
— *ian*	*magician*
— *ist*	*novelist*
— *or*	*surveyor*

2 Suffixes that indicate a person with a particular belief or attitude

— *ian*	*Christian*
— *ist*	*realist*
— *ite*	*Israelite*

3 Suffixes that indicate a place a person is associated with

— *ean*	*European*
— *er*	*New Zealander*
— *ese*	*Vietnamese*
— *i*	*Iraqi*
— *ian*	*Australian*
— *ish*	*Turkish*
— *n*	*Austrian*

4 Suffixes that indicate gender (feminine)

— *e*	*fiancée*
— *ess*	*lioness*

▼ *Suffixes to do with places*

Suffixes that indicate a place for a particular activity

— *age*	*orphanage*
— *arium*	*aquarium*
— *ary*	*veterinary*
— *dom*	*kingdom*
— *ery*	*bakery*
— *orium*	*crematorium*
— *ory*	*observatory*

▼ *Suffixes to do with objects*

Suffixes that indicate an object with a particular purpose

— *er*	*computer*
— *or*	*resistor*

▼ *Suffixes to do with abstract nouns*

1 Suffixes that indicate a condition, accomplishment or state

— *asm*	*enthusiasm*
— *ation*	*occupation*
— *cy*	*bankruptcy*
— *dom*	*freedom*
— *hood*	*childhood*
— *ice*	*justice*
— *ics*	*ethics*
— *ings*	*earnings*
— *ism*	*alcoholism*
— *itis*	*tonsilitis*
— *itude*	*multitude*
— *ment*	*amazement*
— *ness*	*kindness*
— *osis*	*hypnosis*
— *red*	*hatred*
— *ship*	*hardship*
— *ty, ity*	*certainty, vanity*

2 Suffixes that indicate a belief or attitude

— *ism*	*Buddhism*
— *ity*	*Christianity*

3 Suffixes that indicate a process or product

— *age*	*marriage*
— *ion*	*action*

— *ism*	*hypnotism*
— *ment*	*increment*
— *sion*	*tension*
— *tion*	*protection*
— *xion*	*reflexion*

▼ *Suffixes that indicate quantity*

— *age*	*voltage*
— *ful*	*cupful*

▼ *Suffixes that indicate size*

— *cule*	*molecule*
— *et*	*islet*
— *etta*	*operetta*
— *ette*	*cigarette*
— *icle*	*particle*
— *let*	*ringlet*
— *ock*	*hillock*

▼ *Suffixes that indicate plural*

— *a*	*phenomenon/phenomena*
— *ae*	*formula/formulae*
— *en*	*ox/oxen*
— *es*	*baby/babies, tomato/tomatoes, church/churches, wish/wishes, tax/taxes, lass/lasses, thesis/theses*
— *i*	*radius/radii*
— *im*	*cherub/cherubim*
— *s*	*cat/cats, solo/solos*

— *um*	*memorandum/memoranda*
— *x*	*gateau/gateaux*

Suffixes that form adjectives

▼ *Suffixes that often indicate a word is an adjective*

— *ary*	*dietary*
— *ate*	*considerate*
— *eth*	*twentieth*
— *ite*	*favorite*
— *th*	*seventh*
— *ular*	*muscular*

▼ *Suffixes that indicate characteristics*

— *al, ial*	*normal, trivial*
— *ant*	*important*
— *en*	*frozen*
— *ent*	*absorbent*
— *eous*	*gaseous*
— *erly*	*elderly*
— *ern*	*northern*
— *ful*	*wonderful*
— *ic, ical*	*historic*
— *ile*	*fragile*
— *ious*	*ambitious*
— *ive*	*expressive*
— *ly*	*fairly*
— *ous*	*joyous*
— *proof*	*waterproof*
— *y*	*chilly*

▼ *Suffixes that indicate a likeness to something*

— *ed*	pig-headed
— *esque*	statuesque
— *ine*	canine
— *ish*	selfish
— *oid*	spheroid
— *some*	fearsome

▼ *Suffixes that indicate a possible attribute or effect*

— *able*	removable
— *ible*	edible
— *some*	awesome
— *uble*	soluble

▼ *Suffix that indicates a lack of something*

— *less*	careless

▼ *Suffixes that indicate degree*

— *er*	longer
— *est*	longest

Suffixes that form adverbs

▼ *Suffix that indicates an adverb*

— *ly*	quickly

▼ *Suffixes that indicate direction*

— *erly*	easterly
— *ern*	eastern
— *ward, wards*	inward
— *ways*	sideways
— *wise*	clockwise

Suffixes that form verbs

▼ *Suffixes that often indicate a word is a verb*

— *ize, ise*	familiarize/familiarise
— *en*	lighten
— *ate*	concentrate
— *fy*	glorify

▼ *Suffix that indicates the present time*

— *ing*	looking

▼ *Suffix that indicates the past time*

— *ed*	looked

Points to think about

Points to consider when students are learning about suffixes include:

▼ *Introducing suffixes*

Once students have a body of words they recognize and are starting to think about the meaning relationships between words and the construction of words, or are capable of thinking about these relationships, it is appropriate to introduce suffixes. It is also important to consider students' oral vocabulary to ensure they understand the meanings of many words to which a suffix may be added and the change in meaning as a result of adding a suffix, for example, the meaning of *play* compared with *playing*. It is important to remember that the ability of students to form generalizations related to the addition of suffixes to words is dependent upon their experience with suffixes.

Significantly, it must also be remembered that students are not able to form generalizations about the addition of suffixes to base words until they have had multiple encounters with a particular suffix.

▼ *Teaching about suffixes that are relevant to students' writing needs*

There is no particular sequence in which suffixes should be studied. Those students require for their personal writing needs are the suffixes that should be dealt with at any given time. It may be that a suffix is studied on more than one occasion in a particular year level, and it may be that the same suffix is also studied again in subsequent years, depending on the writing needs of the students. It is most likely that this would happen with the suffixes *ing* and *ed*. Generally, when a suffix is studied on more than one occasion it is likely that the words being dealt with will be different words.

▼ *Suffixes indicate parts of speech*

Suffixes indicate the part of speech of a word, such as an adjective, noun or adverb. (Refer to the above list of common suffixes). Other suffixes change the meanings of a word, for example, the suffix *less* in *useless*.

▼ *Suffixes are always spelled the same way*

Suffixes are always spelled the same way. If you know how to spell a suffix in one word it will help you spell other words with that suffix.

▼ *Some base words change when a suffix is added*

Any changes that need to occur when adding a suffix are made to the base word. The suffix is always spelled the same way. For example: *ed*

jumped = jump + *ed*
hopped = hop + *ed* (double the final consonant in *hop* and add *ed*)
saved = save + *ed* (delete the *e* in *save* and add the suffix *ed*)

Generalizations

There are some spelling generalizations that are useful to know as they apply to many words. They are not to be taught to the students as statements to learn by rote memory, but by helping students to notice the way that words are spelled. Students could be encouraged to write statements, *in their own words,* about patterns they observe. The following statements are a guide for teachers so they can draw students' attention to these patterns.

There is no particular order in which generalizations need to be learned. Obviously they would only be introduced when students have enough knowledge of words to be able to notice the connections or patterns. It may take several years to build up a complete understanding of the generalization or to refine the ideas. Be selective about which generalization is appropriate for the class, as observed from their writing, and let their discussion and observations guide what should be dealt with.

▼ *Forming plurals*

When the singular form ends with *s*, *ss*, *ch*, *sh* or *x*, add *es*. For example:

gas — gases, glass — glasses, church — churches, bush — bushes, fox — foxes.
(Exceptions: monarch — monarchs, stomach — stomach.)

When the singular form ends with *consonant* + *y*, change the *y* to *i* and add *es*. For example, fairy — fairies. (Note: not *vowel* +*y*, e.g., boy — boys, chimney — chimneys.)

When the singular form ends with *consonant* + *o*, add *es* and with *vowel* + *o*, add *s*. For example:
• add *es* to the following —

buffalo cargo domino echo flamingo halo hero mango zero mosquito motto memento tomato volcano potato.
(Exceptions: piano solo cello soprano banjo zero silo merino.)

• add *s* to the following —

folio studio portfolio kangaroo radio lassoo rodeo.

For hyphenated words add *s* to the major noun. For example:

passers-by, brothers-in-law, hangers-on, mouse-traps, by-laws, by-ways.

For words ending in *f* or *fe*, change to *ves*. For example, thief — thieves, calf — calves, knife — knives.
(Exceptions: roof — roofs, chief — chiefs, dwarf — dwarfs, handkerchief — handkerchiefs, reef — reefs, wharf — wharfs, gulf — gulfs, cliff — cliffs, bluff — bluffs.)

▼ *Forming comparative and superlative adjectives*
Usually add *er* or *est*, for example, tall — taller, tallest.

For words where the last syllable is a *short vowel* + *consonant,* double the consonant before adding *er* or *est*. For example, fat — fatter, fattest.

For words where the last letter is an *e* delete the e before adding *er* or *est*. For example, large — larger, largest.

For words where the last letters are *consonant* + *y* change the *y* to an *i* before adding *er* or *est*. For example, crazy — crazier, craziest.

▼ *Adding* ing *and* ed
Usually add *ing* or *ed* to the base word. For example, turn — turning, turned.

For words where the last syllable is a *short vowel* + *consonant* and the last syllable is stressed, double the consonant before adding *ing* or *ed*. For example, hop — hopping, hopped, regret — regretting, regretted.

(Note: the consonant is not doubled if the last syllable is not stressed, for example, budget — budgeting, budgeted.)
Exceptions:
• format — formatting, formatted.
• In English, Canadian, Australian and New Zealand publications when the consonant is the letter *l* it is always doubled regardless of whether the first or last syllable of a word is stressed, for example, travel — travelling, travelled. In the U.S.A. the generalization is adhered to.
• In English, Canadian, Australian and New Zealand publications the *p* is doubled in worshipping, worshipped.

For words where the last syllable is *er* or *ur* double the consonant before adding *ing* or *ed*. For example, prefer — preferring, preferred, occur — ocurring, occurred.

For words where the last letter is an *e* delete the e before adding *ing* or *ed*. For example, bake — baking, baked.

For words where the last letters are *consonant* + *y* change the *y* to an *i* before adding *ed*. For example, hurry — hurried, cry — cried.

(Note: This does not apply when adding *ing*, for example, hurry — hurrying, cry — crying.)

▼ *Adding* en
For words such as *write* the e is deleted and the consonant is doubled before adding the *en*. For example, write — written, bite — bitten.

▼ *Adding other suffixes*
For words where the last letters are *consonant* + *y* change the *y* to an *i*

before adding other suffixes. For example:

> beauty — beautiful, beautify, busy — business, try — trier, tries,
> hurry — hurries, happy — happily.
> (Exceptions: shy — shyly, sly — slyly.)

For words ending with a silent *e* drop it when adding suffixes *ant, er, or, ior, iour, ist, ure, ish, ary, al*. For example:

> please — pleasure, pleasant, save — saviour, type — typist,
> blue — bluish, behave — behavior, write — writer, create — creator,
> commune — communal, imagine — imaginary.

For words ending with a silent *e* keep the *e* when adding suffixes *ful, ness, less, ly*. For example, state — stately, hope — hopeless, care — careful. (Exceptions: whole — wholly.)

For words with *ic*, add *al* before adding *ly*. For example, automatic — automatically, economic — economically. (Exception: publicly.)

For words describing direction (north, south, east, west) add *er* before adding *ly*. For example, north — northerly.

For adjectives ending in *ous* drop the *u* when adding *ity* to change to noun form. For example, curious — curiosity, generous — generosity, impetuous — impetuosity.

For words ending in *ic* add *k* before adding the suffixes *er, ing, y, ed*. For example:

> picnic — picnicking, picnicked, picnicker, traffic — trafficked,
> mimic — mimicking, panic — panicky.

▼ Adding prefixes

Prefixes are just added to the beginning of the base word. For example, satisfactory — dissatisfactory, necessary — unnecessary, arranged — prearranged.

Activities

The following activities can be used to help students learn about suffixes:

▼ Developing a class list

As the students discover suffixes when reading or when they begin using them in their writing start a class list of words with suffixes and encourage the students to add to the list as they find others in their reading and writing. Ask the students to underline the suffix in each word and talk with them about what a suffix is, ensuring they understand it is a letter or combination of letters added at the end of a word to form another word.

Using words from the class list demonstrate to the students how the suffixes have been added to the base words by doing word sums similar to the following.

Base word	Suffix		New word
magic	+ian	=	magician
novel	+ist	=	novelist
survey	+or	=	surveyor
love	+ly	=	lovely
wonder	+ful	=	wonderful
guide	+ance	=	guidance
berry	+es	=	berries

Ask the students to explain to each other the meanings of the new words formed when suffixes are added to the base words, for example, *wonderful*. Compare the meanings of these words with the meanings of the base words, in this example, *wonder*.

Explain to the students that a suffix is always spelled the same way and that any changes made when adding a suffix are made to the base word before the suffix is added. In the examples above, changes are made to the base words *guide* and *berry* before the suffixes are added. The letter *e* is deleted from the word *guide* and the letter *y* is changed to an *i* in the word *berry* and then the suffixes added to form the new words *guidance* and *berries* respectively. Ask the students to think about how knowing this will help them when they are writing.

▼ Classifying suffixes

As the class list of suffixes develops assist the students to classify the words according to their suffixes, for example, all words ending with the suffix *ly* would be grouped together. Start a class chart for each suffix and encourage the students to add words that they find in their personal writing or reading to the lists.

Choose one suffix to focus on, this being the one that will be most useful for the students to know about for their personal writing, for example *ing*. Ask students to search for words containing *ing*. Again, they could search their personal writing, class charts, topic lists and reading materials. Ask them to think about the meaning of the suffix *ing* and the way it is spelled consistently in each word, and to observe whether or not the spelling of the base word changes when the suffix *ing* is added.

Continue to talk with the students about how knowing about suffixes will assist them when they are attempting to spell unknown words in their writing. Repeat the above procedure with other suffixes on the class list or which occur in the students' writing.

▼ Publishing a class book

Assist the students to publish a class book of suffixes. This could consist of the collated class charts or it may be a separate publication. Involve the students in deciding on the organization of the book. A contents page could be included for easy reference. Students may also like to include a page on which they each write something that they have learned about the different suffixes and how this will assist them with their writing. Alternatively, it may be suitable to publish a special book for one suffix, for example, the suffix *ing*. The published book could be placed in the class library for the students to refer to or borrow.

Our book about the suffix "*ing*"

Some words from our reading and writing that contain the suffix "ing".

* Adding "ing" to one syllable words with a short vowel before the final letter.

* Adding "ing" to one syllable words where there is not a short vowel before the final letter.

* Adding "ing" to words that end in "e"

* Adding "ing" to words of two or more syllables.

* Adding "ing" to words that end in "y."

A class book that focuses exclusively on the suffix **ing**. *The Year 4 students are learning about the changes made to base words when adding the suffix* **ing**.

▼ *Students selecting words to learn*

Some of the words students select to learn may end with a suffix, for example, *actor*, with the suffix *or*. It is useful to list other words that contain the same suffix for students to learn, for example, *sculptor, extractor, illustrator, indicator* and to discuss with them why these other words have been listed. It is important that students understand that if they can spell a suffix in one word they can spell it in other words and that they therefore have a great deal of power when using the English written language.

▼ *Further clarifying understandings about suffixes*

Students may conduct a word search for words containing a particular suffix, for example, *ment*. These words could then be added to a class list or book. During this activity some students may list words where the letters *ment* do not form a suffix, for example, in the word *cement*. When this occurs demonstrate to the students why the string of letters *ment* is not a suffix on this occasion, by separating the word in the following way — *ce + ment*. In this way students can see that *ce* is not a base word and therefore *ment* is not a suffix in the word *cement*. Ask them to think about how this knowledge will assist them when they attempt to spell unknown words in their writing and encourage the students to review and refine their generalizations about the suffix as they find it in other words. See pages 91–93 for more information about generalizations.

▼ *Students complete activities with suffixes*

It may become apparent during discussions with students or from reading their writing that further clarification of their understandings about suffixes is necessary. If this is so, students could complete activities similar to the following and could also create such activities for their peers to complete. The words selected for the activities should be taken from class lists, students' writing and reading materials, lists of words they have selected to learn, topic lists, and other sources that are relevant to them.

Note: The activities described below for adding suffixes to form comparatives and superlatives, and the plural form of words may be used with any suffix. The starting point when teaching about a particular suffix would be dictated by the writing needs of the students at any given time. It may be that adding suffixes to words that end in *e* is taught before adding a suffix to a word where there is no change in the base word. It is important that students learn about adding a particular suffix to words with different endings or different numbers of syllables. For example:

If teaching students about suffixes that form comparatives and superlatives the following could be taught:

- adding *er* and *est* to a word where there is no change to the base word
- adding *er* and *est* to a single syllable word where the final consonant is doubled
- adding *er* and *est* to a word that ends with *e*
- adding *er* and *est* to a word that ends with *y*

Since all activities students complete should be highly relevant to their writing needs, it is important not to ask students to practise more examples than is necessary for them to understand the concept being taught. Consequently, some students may grasp the concept after one or two attempts and therefore do not require further practice.

1   Students focus on suffixes that form the comparative and superlative forms of words, that is, the suffixes *er* and *est*.

Example 1

Complete this comparative and superlative table by adding the suffixes *er* and *est* or by writing the base word. If necessary check your spellings in a dictionary or wordbook.

Base Word	Comparative	Superlative
sweet	....	....
....	....	old<u>est</u>
poor	....	....
....	....	new<u>est</u>
....	soon<u>er</u>	....

Ask the students to think about why there are no changes to the base word in these examples before adding the suffixes *er* and *est*. To assist them, when it is appropriate, draw attention to the following features of the words above:

- where the letter before the final consonant is a vowel, it is not a short vowel
- or the letter before the final consonant is a consonant.

Ask them how knowing about this will assist them when writing the comparative and superlative forms of words.

Example 2

Complete the comparative and superlative table below by adding the suffixes *er* and *est* to the following words. If necessary check your spellings in a dictionary or wordbook.

	Comparative	**Superlative**
wet	....	....
hot	....	....
red	....	....

Write a generalization in your own words about the changes you made to the base words *wet*, *hot* and *red* to form their comparative and superlative forms.

....

....

....

Talk with the students about their generalizations and encourage them to review them periodically as they encounter other words with the same suffixes. Ask them to think about how knowing when to double the final consonant when adding suffixes that form the comparative and superlative will assist them when writing.

If necessary assist the students to compare the examples in Example 1 with those in Example 2.

Example 3

Students add the suffixes *er* and *est* to words that end in *e*.

Here are some words that end in *e* with their comparative and superlative forms.

Base word	**Comparative**	**Superlative**
pale	pal<u>er</u>	pal<u>est</u>
idle	idl<u>er</u>	idl<u>est</u>
huge	hug<u>er</u>	hug<u>est</u>
game	gam<u>er</u>	gam<u>est</u>

Which letter do the base words end with? ....

What change has been made to the base word before the suffixes *er* and *est* have been added?

Talk with the students about their understandings and encourage them to review their generalizations periodically. Ask them to think about how knowing how to add the suffixes *er* and *est* to words that end in *e* will assist them when writing.

Wednesday 2nd september
We comeper words
and put er on the end
or est on the end for
fat and small

The above generalization is written in the student's own words. As this student in Year 2 learns more about forming comparatives and superlatives the above generalization should be reviewed and refined.

Demonstrate to the students how they can apply their generalizations to complete the following comparative and superlative table. Select words from their writing and encourage them to check their spellings in a dictionary or wordbook if necessary.

Base word	Comparative	Superlative
wise	....	....
fine	....	....
....	tamer	....

Ask the students to review the work they have completed and write a generalization about what they did when changing words that end in *e* to their comparative and superlative forms.

Example 4
Students add the suffixes *er* and *est* to words that end in *y*.

Complete the following comparative and superlative table. Note that all of the base words end with *y*. If necessary check your spellings in a dictionary or wordbook.

Base word	Comparative	Superlative
juicy	....	....
....	lazier	....
funny	....	funniest
....	wealthier	....

Ask the students to review the work they have completed and write a generalization about what they did when changing words that end in *y* to form their comparative and superlative forms.

Talk with the students about their understandings and encourage them to review their generalizations periodically. Ask them to think about how knowing how to add the suffixes *er* and *est* to words that end in *y* will assist them when writing.

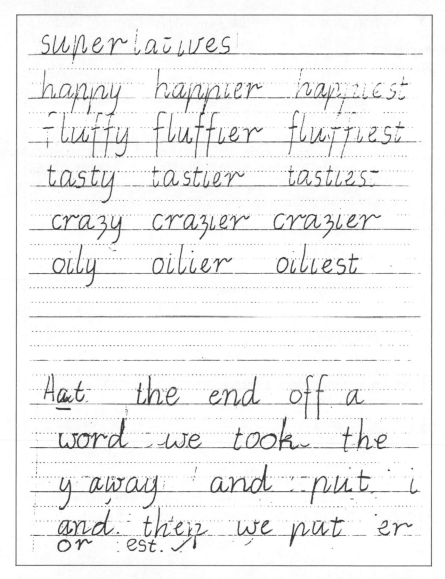

superlatives

happy happier happiest
fluffy fluffier fluffiest
tasty tastier tastiest
crazy crazier crazier
oily oilier oiliest

Aat the end off a word we took the y away and put i and then we put er or est.

Students in Year 3 write base words, comparatives and superlatives and write a generalization about what they did in their own words.

▼ *Students focus on suffixes that form the plural forms of words*

Example 1
Students add the suffix *es* to form the plural.

The plural forms of some words are made by adding *es*. For example:

fox — foxes   church — churches   dish — dishes
bus — buses   loss — losses

Notice that the words above end in *x*, *ch*, *sh*, *s* or *ss*. Use this information to complete the following table. If necessary use a dictionary or wordbook to help you.

Singular	Plural
torch	....
guess	....
....	flashes
....	boxes
gas	....
....	ashes
hippopotamus	....
....	kisses

Write a generalization about what happens when you add the suffix *es* to a word to write its plural form.

....
....
....

Talk with the students about their understandings and encourage them to review their generalizations periodically. Ask them to think about how knowing how to form plurals by adding the suffix *es* will assist them when writing.

Example 2
Students add the suffixes *es* and *s* to form the plurals of words that end in *y*.

Look at the words below that end in *y*. They are written in both their singular and plural forms:

Consonant + y	Vowel + y
berry — berries	boy — boys
baby — babies	bay — bays
daisy — daisies	tray — trays

The words in the first column end with *consonant* + *y*. How have these words been changed to their plural forms?

....
....

The words in the second column end with *vowel* + *y*. How have these words been changed to their plural forms?

....
....

Can you make a general statement about the plural forms of words that end in the letter *y*?

....
....
....

Talk with the students about their understandings and encourage them to review their generalizations periodically. Ask them to think about how knowing how to form the plurals of words that end in *y* will assist them when writing.

Example 3

Students add suffixes to form the plurals of words that end in /f/.

> The words *dwarf* and *elf* both end with the /f/ sound. Write the plural forms of these words. Use a dictionary or wordbook to help you.
>
> dwarf .... elf ....
>
> Notice that the plurals of these words are formed differently.
> You have probably noticed in your reading and writing that words that end with the /f/ sound change to the plural form in the following way:
>
> > dwarf — dwarfs; giraffe — giraffes (add *s*)
> > wolf — wolves (change the *f* to *v* and add *es*)
> > wife — wives (change the *f* to *v* and add *s*)
>
> Change these words into their plural form. Use a dictionary or wordbook to check your spellings.
> calf .... half .... life ....
> leaf .... thief .... self ....
>
> What do you notice about the words that end with the /f/ sound? Write some generalizations about what happens to words ending with the /f/ sound when their plural form is written.
>
> ....
> ....
> ....

Talk with the students about their understandings and encourage them to review their generalizations periodically. Ask them to think about how knowing how to form the plural of words that end in the /f/ sound will assist them when writing.

▼ *Students focus on the suffix* ly

Students add the suffix *ly* to words.

Example 1

> Notice how the words *quietly*, *lightly* and *quickly* are formed by adding the suffix *ly* to each base word.
>
> quiet + ly = quiet<u>ly</u>   light + ly – light<u>ly</u>   quick + ly – quick<u>ly</u>
>
> Here are some other words that contain the suffix *ly*. Underline the suffix *ly* in each word and complete the word sums. The first one has been done for you.
>
> slow<u>ly</u>   = slow + ly   smoothly   = ... + ...
> roughly = ... + ...   really   = ... + ...
> ideally = ... + ...   thoughtfully = ... + ...
>
> Now add the suffix *ly* to the following words to form new words:
>
> curious + ly = ...   real + ly = ...
> faint + ly = ...   faithful + ly = ...
> final + ly = ...   near + ly = ...
>
> Were any changes made to the base words before adding the suffix *ly*? ....
> What do you notice about the words *really, ideally, finally, faithfully* and *thoughtfully*? Talk with a friend about the reason these words have *ll*.
>
> Complete the following statement in your own words about what happens when the suffix *ly* is added to base words.
> When the suffix *ly* is added to a base word ....
> ....

Talk with the students about their generalizations and encourage them to review these periodically. Ask them to think about how knowing how to add the suffix *ly* will assist them when writing.

▼ *Crosswords*

Many games may be played using suffixes, for example, crosswords. Note how the clues have been written as spelling clues.

Across

5 poor + ly =
6 merry + ly =
8 quiet + ly =
9 happy + ly =
11 rare + ly =

Down

1 occasional + ly =
2 frequent + ly =
3 nice + ly =
4 rough + ly =
7 thorough + ly =

14 patient + ly =
15 quick + ly =
16 careful + ly=
17 love + ly =
18 sad + ly =

10 immediate + ly =
12 final + ly =
13 slow + ly=

Refer to Chapter 11 for other suitable games.

Word families

A word family is a group of words that are related in meaning. Each word in the word family is derived from the same base word but has had different prefixes and/or suffixes added to it. For example:

> **Base word — cover**
> Prefixes such as *un, re* and *dis* can be added to *cover* to form the words *uncover, recover, discover.*
> Suffixes such as *s, ing* and *ed* can be added to *cover* to form the words *covers, covering, covered.*
> Prefixes and suffixes can both be added to *cover* to form words such as *recovers, uncovered,* and so on.

Knowing that each word in the word family *cover* is related in meaning will help writers to spell many other words in the same word family.

Note: It was not considered useful to provide a list of word families.

Points to think about

Points to consider when students are learning about word families include:

▼ *Introducing word families*

Once students have a body of words they recognize and they are starting to think about the meaning relationships between words in a word family, or are capable of thinking about these relationships, it is appropriate to introduce word families. It is also important to consider the development of students' oral vocabulary to ensure they understand the meanings of several words within a word family.

▼ *Knowing about the meaning relationships between words gives writers power when using the English written language*

If you can spell one word in a word family there are many other words in the same word family that you can spell. For example, if you know how to spell *soft* you can spell other words in the *soft* word family, such as *soften* and *softening*, even though the words are pronounced differently.

▼ *Sometimes changes are made to a base word when suffixes are added*

Sometimes a change is made to the base word in a word family when a suffix is added. For example, in words that end in *e*, such as *like*, the *e* is dropped before adding the suffix *ing* — *like* + *ing* = *liking*, and in words that end in *y* the *y* is changed to an *i* before the suffix *ed* is added, for example, *satisfy* + *ed* = *satisfied*. For more information about generalizations that apply when adding suffixes to words refer to pages 91 to 93.

Activities

These activities can be used to help students learn about word families:

▼ *Developing class lists*

As students discover words from the same word family when reading or when they begin using them in their writing start class lists of these words. When listing words in a word family ensure the students understand their meanings and that they are words they are likely to use in their writing. Encourage the students to add to the word family lists as they find other words from the respective word families or as they think of other words by adding prefixes and suffixes. Ensure the students understand a word family is a group of words that are related in meaning — prefixes and suffixes are added to a base word to change or add to its meaning.

Using an example from the class lists of word families demonstrate how prefixes and suffixes have been added to a base word, by doing word sums similar to the following. For example:

Prefix	Base word	Suffix	Words in *play* word family
re +	play		= replay
	play	+ ful	= playful
	play	+ er	= player
	play	+ ing	= playing
re +	play	+ ed	= replayed

Ask the students to explain to each other the meanings of the new words formed when prefixes and suffixes are added to the base word *play*, for example, *replay* and *player*. Compare the meanings of these words with the other words in the word family *play*. Ask students to think about how knowing about word families will help them when attempting to spell unknown words in their writing.

governing
government
governed
parliament
parliamentry
parliament house
parliamentarian
parliaments
parliamentarians
politician
politics
magic
magician
politicise
polity
politica + economical
politicing
politically
politico – economica

In the word politics you could sound it out but that would be different with politician because you cant really hear the *a* sound, when you say the word Government you cant hear the silent N.

A Year 6 class was studying the topic **politics**. *The students frequently misspelled the words* **politician** *and* **government** *so the teacher developed class lists of related words and discussed the meaning relationships between them. The students learned that knowing how to spell one word would enable them to spell others in the same word family.*

A Year 6 student demonstrates her understanding of the meaning relationships between words and how understanding this will help her with her spelling.

▼ *Students selecting words to learn*

When students are selecting words to learn it may be appropriate to also list other words in the same word family. For example, if a student chose to learn the word *magic*, it would be useful to add other words from the *magic* word family to be learned, such as *magician, magicians* and *magical*. Ask the students to think about how this will help them with their writing.

When learning words it is important students do not learn them in isolation but in relationship to other words.

▼ *Students complete activities with word families*

The words selected for the activities should be taken from class lists, students' writing and reading materials, lists of words they have selected to learn, topic lists, and other sources that are relevant to them.

1 This activity focuses on the meaning and spelling relationships that exist between words in the same word family. Students add words from a list to a group of words from the same word family. For example:

---

soft   sweet   like   eat   chew   lunch

Add each word from above to its word family below and write some other words that belong to the same word family. Use a dictionary or wordbook to help you. Underline the base word that is the same in each word as shown.

...................., chewing, <u>chew</u>ed, ...

...................., <u>lunch</u>es, play <u>lunch</u>, ...

...................., <u>lik</u>ing, <u>lik</u>ed, dis<u>lik</u>e, ...

...................., <u>soft</u>er, <u>soft</u>est, <u>soft</u>en, ...

...................., <u>eat</u>en, <u>eat</u>ing, ...

...................., <u>sweet</u>er, <u>sweet</u>est, un<u>sweet</u>ened, ...

Talk with the students about how knowing about the meaning relationship between words in word families will help them with spelling.

2 Adding prefixes and suffixes to a base word to form other words in the same word family. This activity focuses on the meaning and spelling relationships that exist between words in the same word family. For example:

The word *occupation* belongs to the same word family as *occupy*. Write other words in the family by adding different prefixes and suffixes to the base word *occupy*.

un + occupy + ed = unoccupied

un	occupy	ed
pre		ing
re		ant
		ation al
		er
		s

Ask the students how knowing about word families will assist them when they are writing.

Compound words

A compound word is a word formed from two or more smaller words. The meaning of a compound word is related to the meaning of the smaller words within it — a compound word is not just two or more words put together.

Note: It was not considered useful to provide a list of compound words.

Points to think about

Points to consider when students are learning about compound words include:

▼ *Introducing compound words*

Once students have a body of words they recognize and they are starting to use compound words in their writing, or they are able to think about the relationships of the smaller words in the compound word to the meaning of the compound word itself, it is appropriate to introduce compound words. It is also important to consider the development of students' oral vocabulary to ensure they understand the meanings of compound words that may be formed.

▼ *The meanings of compound words*

The meaning of a compound word is the total of the meanings of the smaller words within it, for example *birthday* means the *day* of *birth*.

▼ *Knowing about the spelling of compound words gives writers power when using the English written language*

Knowing how to spell the smaller words that form a compound word, for example *over* and *board*, enables writers to spell compound words, in this case, *overboard*. Conversely, knowing how to spell a compound word means writers can also spell the smaller words in it and can thus spell many other words containing the smaller words. Using the above example, if students know how to spell *over* in *overboard* it will help them to spell other compound words that contain *over*, such as *overthrow, overdue* and *overrule*.

▼ *Knowing about the three types of compound words*

There are three types of compound words. For example:

- Closed: *breakfast* (the two smaller words *break* and *fast* form one whole word).
- Open: *milk shake* (the two smaller words *milk* and *shake* are separated by a space).
- Hyphenated: *twenty-five* (the two smaller words *twenty* and *five* are joined by a hyphen).

When proofreading their writing students may find it necessary to check a dictionary or wordbook to determine whether a compound word is closed, open or hyphenated. As a result of consulting various dictionaries students may find that the same word is written in different ways in the different dictionaries, for example, hyphenated or open. If this occurs students can discuss their findings and decide which version they wish to use in their personal writing. Discuss with the students the importance of using a consistent form, for example, hyphenated (egg-plant) or not hyphenated (eggplant), in their personal writing.

▼ *Compound words may be formed from several smaller words*

Compound words may be formed from two or more smaller words. For example:

sunshine (sun + shine) — two words
mother-in-law (mother + in + law) — three words
jack-in-the-box (jack + in + the + box) — four words

Activities

The following activities can be used to help students learn about compound words:

▼ *Developing a class list*

As students discover compound words when reading and writing begin a class list. When listing compound words ensure the students understand their meanings and that they are words they are likely to use in their writing. Talk with them about how knowing how to spell the smaller words, for example, *cup* and *board* enables them to spell the compound word *cupboard*. Talk with them about the meaning relationship between the smaller words within the compound word and the compound word itself. In this case the original meaning of the word *cupboard* was a *board* on which a *cup* was placed.

Conversely, demonstrate to the students how knowing how to spell a compound word, for example, *lighthouse* means that they can spell the smaller words *light* and *house* within that compound word. Explain that if they can spell the words *light* and *house* in *lighthouse* it means they can spell those words in other words, such as *light-hearted* and *houseboat*. Talk with the students about how this will assist them when they are attempting to spell unknown words when they are writing.

```
playground
play dough
play time
play-mate
play-mates
playgrounds
playpen
playpens
play-group

play + ground = playground
play + ground = playground
play + time = playtime
play + mate = playmate
play + pen = playpen
play + grounds = playgrounds
```

Year 2 class forming compound words based on the word **play**.

If you can spell 'play' in one word
you can ... Spell a lot of words with play
in them

played ✓   ✓ re playing
playing ✓   ✓ replayer.
playmate ✓   ✓ replay
playpen ✓   ✓ playgroup
playtime ✓   ✓ play dough
playgrounds ✓   ✓ replay's
playground ✓   ✓ players
playful ✓
replayed ✓

The Year 2 class went on to discover what other words they could spell if they could spell **play***.*

▼ Publishing a class book

Assist the students to publish a book of compound words. This could consist of the collated class charts or it may be a separate publication. Involve the students in deciding on the organization of the book, for example, the compound words could be arranged according to the number of smaller

words in them or alphabetically. If the words are arranged alphabetically it would allow compound words that contain the same smaller words to be grouped together, for example, *bookshelf* and *bookmark* would appear on the *b* page.

The book could have a contents page and the students may also like to include a page on which they each write something that they have learned about compound words. Place the book in the class library for the students to refer to or borrow.

▼ Students searching for compound words

Students could be asked to conduct a word search for compound words. They could search class topic lists, class spelling lists, dictionaries, wordbooks, their personal writing and personal reading materials.

For example, if your class was working on the topic *School* the words below may be listed during a brainstorm. These words can then provide a source for learning about the relationships that exist between words in the English written language, in this case, compound words. For further information about topic lists refer to pages 23–25. For example:

Class topic list - school

playground classroom headmaster
principal vice-principal white-
board classmate secretary
mathematics reading lesson
teacher test mark white-
out practice gymnasium
recess sickbay library chalk
blackboard classroom bookcases
desk bookshelves book notebook
dictionary

Year 2 students were studying the topic **School***. This topic list became the basis for many spelling activities where words with common features, for example, compound words and high frequency words were studied.*

To assist students to develop their understandings about compound words they could complete activities similar to the following, using words from the topic list on the previous page.

---

1 Write the compound words in the list above.

....

....

....

2 Write the compound words that contain the word *book*.

....

Write other compound words you can think of that contain the word *book* (use a dictionary or wordbook to help you).

....

3 Write the compound words that contain the words *board, white* and *class*.

....

....

4 Write other compound words you can think of that contain the words *play, board* and *white* (use a dictionary or wordbook to help you).

play...

board...

white..

Ask the students to think about how these activities will assist them when they are attempting to spell unknown words in their writing.

▼   *Students complete activities with compound words*

To clarify students' understandings about compound words activities similar to the following could be completed. The words used in the activity could be taken from class lists, words students have selected to learn, students' writing or materials that they are reading.

1   Students may be asked to combine single words from two columns to form compound words. For example:

Find a word from column 1 and from column 2 that form a compound word in column 3. Write the two parts with the compound word on the lines below, for example: *tea + cake = teacake*. If you are not sure of the meaning of a word ask a friend or check in a dictionary.

Column 1	Column 2	Column 3
tea	nut	meat loaf
fish	*cake*	fish paste
dough	crumbs	fruit salad
meat	loaf	doughnut
bread	salad	breadcrumbs
fruit	paste	teacake
tea	+ cake	= teacake

.... + ... = ...

.... + ... = ...

.... + ... = ...

.... + ... = ...

When students have completed this activity they could then take the smaller words and list other compound words that contain them, for example, *milk bar, fishhook* and *fruit-fly*.

Ask them to think about how knowing that if they can spell one word they can spell many others and how this will assist them when they are attempting to spell unknown words in their writing.

2   Students select some compound words, separate them into the smaller words and then use each smaller word to make other compound words. For example: **teacake**

tea teapot, **tea**cup, **tea**time, **tea**-leaf, **tea**-table, **tea**-caddy, **tea**-break, **tea**spoon, **tea**-tree, **tea**-towel
cake cake shop, fish **cake**, potato **cake**

The smaller word that is used repeatedly in the compound words could be underlined. Talk with the students about how knowing that if they can spell one word they can spell many others and how this will assist them when they are writing.

3 Students create activities for others to complete

Compound staircase

Students could choose suitable compound words as the starting point for compound staircases for each other to complete. They may need to refer to a dictionary or wordbook for suitable words. Students could also search their writing or reading materials for examples of compound words, for example, *moonlight*. A compound staircase could be built by using the second part of the compound word as the first part of the next compound word. For example:

shoeshine

horseshoe

race horse

boat race

houseboat

lighthouse

moonlight

The students should talk with each other about how this activity will assist them with their writing.

4 Playing games with compound words. If it becomes apparent during discussions with students or from reading their writing that further clarification of their understandings about compound words is necessary, the students could play some of the games in Chapter 11 using compound words.

▼ *Compound words and the 100 common words*

The 100 common words are very useful words for students to know how to spell, considering that these words account for approximately 50 per cent of words writers use. For further information see page 15.

To demonstrate to students how frequently they use some words when writing, give each student a list of the 100 common words and ask them to review their recent pieces of writing and mark each time they have used a word from this list. Discuss the frequency of use of various words and ask the students to check their spellings of the commonly used words.

If students misspell some of the words from the common word list, for example, *every*, it may be appropriate to include these words in compound word activities. For example:

---

1 Make compound words by combining *every* with the words below:

thing ....

where ....

every + day ....

body ....

one ....

2 Make compound words by combining *one* with the words below.

any ....

no + *one* ....

some ....

every ....

Note: When doing this activity the smaller word to be used more than once when forming new compound words may be the first or the second smaller word in the compound word.

A Year 1 student using words from the 100 common words list to form compound words.

Ask the students to think about how knowing that if they can spell one word, such as *every*, they can spell many other words containing *every*, and how this will assist them when they are writing.

▼ *Students selecting words to learn*

Some of the words students select to learn may be compound words, for example, *raincoat*. When this occurs it is useful to also list other compound words with the smaller words *rain* and *coat*, such as *rainbow, rainforest, rainfall* or *coathanger* for the students to learn. Talk with the students about how knowing that if they can spell one word they can spell many others and how this will assist them when they are attempting to spell unknown words in their writing.

▼ *Understanding why some compound words have double letters*

As students find examples of compound words with double letters, for example *rr* in the compound word *overrule*, ask them to explain why this occurs when double letters do not exist in either of the smaller words *over* or *rule*. To assist them demonstrate how the two words *over* and *rule* combine to form *overrule*. Ensure they understand that if, for example, one word within the compound word ends in *r (over)* and the other word within the compound word begins with *r (rule)* double letters will occur. The students can provide similar explanations for other cases where the doubling of letters occurs. Talk with the students about how this will assist them when they are attempting to spell unknown words in their writing.

▼ *Further clarifying the concept of a compound word*

As a result of a word search for compound words students may have listed words that are not compound words, for example, *legend*. When this occurs demonstrate to the students why *legend* is not a compound word, even though it consists of two smaller words, *leg* and *end*. (The meaning of the word *legend* is not related in meaning to the smaller words *leg* and *end*). Repeat this procedure with other words students have listed incorrectly.

A double-page spread in a Year 2 student's spelling book where he writes in his own words what he understands about compound words.

Creating Words

Acronyms

An acronym is a word formed by joining together the first letters of other words.

Below is a list of common acronyms. This list is provided as a resource of the range of acronyms and it is not intended as a list of words to be learned.

Actil	*Australian Cotton Textile Industries Limited*
AIDS	*Acquired Immune Deficiency Syndrome*
ALCAN	*Aluminium Company of Canada*
Alcoa	*Aluminium Company of America*
Anzac	*Australian and New Zealand Army Corps*
ANZUS	*Australia, New Zealand and the United States*
ASEAN	*Association of South East Asian Nations*
AWOL	*Absent Without Leave*
BASIC	*Beginner's All-purpose Symbolic Instruction Code*
Bass	*Best Available Seating Services, Australia Pty Ltd*
cad	*computer-assisted design*
cal	*computer-assisted learning*
Chogm	*Commonwealth Heads of Government Meeting*
IATA	*International Air Transport Association*
Ibby	*International Board of Books for Young People*
Ipec	*Interstate Parcel Express Company*
laser	*light amplification by stimulated emission of radiation*
maser	*microwave amplification by stimulated emission of radiation*
MASH	*Mobile Army Surgical Hospital*
NASA	*National Aeronautics and Space Administration*
NATO	*North Atlantic Treaty Organization*
OPEC	*Organization of Petroleum Exporting Countries*
Pakistan	*Punjab, Afghan, Kashmir, Sind, Tan (Baluchistan)*
PAYE	*pay as you earn (tax)*
Pin	*Personal Identification Number*
Qantas	*Queensland and Northern Territory Aerial Services*
radar	*radio detection and ranging*
Rosta	*Road Safety and Traffic Authority*
rem	*rapid eye movement*
Safcol	*South Australian Fish Co-operative Limited*
SAL	*Surface Air Lift*
SALT	*Strategic Arms Limitation Talks*
SAM	*surface to air missile*
scuba	*self-contained underwater breathing apparatus*
SEATO	*South-East Asia Treaty Organization*
snafu	*situation normal, all fouled up*

sonar	*sound navigation (and) ranging*
UNESCO	*United Nations Educational, Scientific and Cultural Organization*
UNICEF	*United Nations International Children's Emergency Fund*
WASP	*White Anglo-Saxon Protestant*
WHO	*World Health Organization*
wowser	*We only want social evils remedied*

Points to think about

Points to consider when students are learning about acronyms include:

▼ *Introducing acronyms*

Once students have a body of words they recognize and they are starting to think about the meaning relationships between words, or are capable of thinking about these relationships, it is appropriate to introduce acronyms. It is also important to consider the development of students' oral vocabulary to ensure they understand the meanings of the words from which the acronyms originate.

▼ *The pronunciation of acronyms*

Acronyms are usually pronounced as a single word. They may be made up of capital letters *(UNESCO)* or lower case letters *(radar)*. When the use of lower case letters may be confused with another word, for example *SALT* or *WHO*, upper case letters are used. Acronyms that are formed from the names of companies, organizations and other bodies may have an initial capital letter only *(Qantas)*. Acronyms do not have full stops between letters or at the end of the word.

▼ *The origin of acronyms*

The spelling of an acronym is determined by the first letters of the words from which it is formed and knowing the origin of an acronym can help students to learn its spelling.

▼ *Introducing words into the English language*

The forming of acronyms is one way words are introduced into the English language.

▼ *Qantas is an acronym*

The word *Qantas* does not have the letter *u* following *q* because it is an acronym.

▼ *The use of acronyms*

Many acronyms are related to the areas of computers, science and the defence forces.

Activities

The following activities can be used to help students learn about acronyms:

▼ *Developing a class list*

When the students discover acronyms in their reading and writing assist them to develop a class list and encourage them to add to the list as they find other acronyms. It would be useful to include on the class list the acronyms and the words from which they are formed. When listing acronyms ensure the students understand their meanings and that they are words they are likely to use in their writing. For example:

scuba	self-contained underwater breathing apparatus
Qantas	Queensland and Northern Territory Aerial Services
Anzac	Australian and New Zealand Army Corps

Continue to demonstrate to students the relationship that exists between acronyms and the words from which they are derived. Ask the students to think about how this will assist them when they are writing.

▼ *Publishing a big book*

When the students have listed a reasonable number of acronyms assist them to publish a big book. The acronyms could be arranged according to the topic they relate to, for example, *sonar* and *radar* could be under the heading of communication, while *Actil, ALCAN* and *Alcoa* could be under the heading of companies. The book could have a contents page and be placed in the class library for the students to refer to or borrow.

Resources

Jones, David (comp.), *The Australian dictionary of acronymns and abbreviations*, Second Back Row Press, Leura, NSW, 1981.
Pugh, E A., *A Dictionary of Acronyms and Abbreviations*, Clive Bingley, London, 1970.

Blended words (Portmanteau words)

A blended word is often formed by blending the start of one word with the end of another word. A blended word has the same meaning as the meanings of the two words from which it originated.

Below is a list of common blended words. This list is provided as a resource of the range of blended words and it is not intended as a list of words to be learned.

Blend	Source
aerosol	aero + solution
aerobatics	aero + acrobatics
Amex	American Express
bedsit	bedroom + sitting room

Blend	Source
bit	binary digit
bookmobile	books + automobile
breathalyzer	breath + analyzer
brunch	breakfast + lunch
cablegram	cable + telegram
camiknickers	camisole + knickers
chortle	chuckle + snort
Cinerama	cinema + panorama
cosmonaut	cosmo + astronaut
Dictaphone	dictate + phone
Dictograph	dictation + o + graph
electrocute	electro + execute
Eurailpass	European Railway Passenger
Eurasia	Europe + Asia
Eurovision	European + television
gerrymander	Gerry + salamander
Gestapo	Gheime + Staatpolizei
guesstimate	guess + estimate
heliport	helicopter + airport
hi-fi	high + fidelity
Identikit	Identification + kit
Intelsat	International + Consortium + for + Telecommunications + Satellite
intercom	inter + communication
Interpol	International + Criminal + Police + Commission
Mediaid	medical + aid
Medibank	medical + bank
Medicare	medical + care
methedrine	methyl + benzedrine
modem	modulation + demodulation
moped	motor + pedal bike
motel	motor + hotel
moto-cross	motor cycles + cross country

Blend	Source
motorcade	*motor cars + cavalcade*
Nabisco	*National + Biscuit + Company*
newscast	*news + broadcast*
Oxfam	*Oxford (Committee for) Famine Relief*
paratroops	*parachute + troops*
pedicab	*pedal + i + cab*
picalilli	*pickle + al + chilli*
polocrosse	*polo + lacrosse*
Prestel	*press + television or press + telephone*
prissy	*prim + sissy*
ruckus	*ruction + k + rumpus*
sci-fi	*science + fiction*
simulcast	*simultaneous + broadcast*
sitcom	*situation + comedy*
smaze	*smoke + haze*
smog	*smoke + fog*
splotch	*spot + blotch*
stodge	*stuff + podge*
talkathon	*talk + marathon*
telecast	*television + broadcast*
telethon	*television + marathon*
telex	*teleprinter + exchange*
trafficator	*traffic + indicator*
transistor	*transfer + resistor*
travelogue	*travel + catalogue*
twiddle	*twist/twirl + fiddle*
twirl	*twist + whirl*
walkathon	*walk + marathon*

Points to think about

Points to consider when students are learning about blended words include:

▼ *Introducing blended words*

Once students have a body of words they recognize and they are starting to think about the meaning relationships between words, or are capable of thinking about these relationships, it is appropriate to introduce blended words. It is also important to consider the development of students' oral vocabulary to ensure they understand the meanings of the words from which the blended words originate.

▼ *The spellings and meanings of blended words*

The spelling of a blended or portmanteau word is related to the spelling of the words from which it is formed. The meaning of a portmanteau word is related to the meanings of the words from which it is formed. Demonstrate to students how knowing the spelling of the words from which blended words are formed will assist them when attempting to spell portmanteau words in their own writing. This is even more relevant if students create blended words of their own, such as *ginormous* from *gigantic* and *enormous*.

▼ *Introducing new words to the English language*

The English language is a living language and new words are constantly being introduced. The creation of blended words is one way new words enter the language.

▼ *The meaning of the word portmanteau*

A portmanteau is a leather case that opens into two parts. Relate this to the term *portmanteau word* which is an invented word that combines the sounds and meanings of two or more other words.

Activities

These activities can be used to help students learn about blended words:

▼ *Developing a class list*

As students discover blended words in their reading and writing assist them to develop a class list of blended words and the words they originate from. Encourage students to add to the list as they find other examples of blended words in their reading and writing. When listing blended words ensure the students understand their meanings and that they are words they are likely to use in their writing. Talk with the students about how knowing about the meaning relationship that exists between blended words and the words from which they are derived will assist them in their writing.

▼ *Publishing a class book*

When the students have listed a reasonable number of blended words assist them to publish a class book. This could be collated class charts or a separate publication. Involve the students in deciding on the organization of the book. A contents page could be included for easy reference. Students may also like to include a page on which they each write something that they have learned about the spellings and meanings of blended words. Place the book in the class library.

▼ *Playing games with blended words*

It may become apparent during discussions with students or from reading their writing that further clarification of their understandings about blended words is necessary. If this is so, students could play some of the games in Chapter 11 using blended words. The words selected should be taken from class lists, students' writing and reading materials, lists of words they have selected to learn, topic lists, and so on.

Eponyms

Eponyms are words that originate from the names of people, places or institutions.

Below is a list of common eponyms. This list is provided as a resource of the range of eponyms. It is not intended as a list of words to be learned.

▼ *Words originating from people's names*

Eponym	Source
Achilles Heel	*Achilles (hero in* The Iliad*)*
Adonis	*Adonis (Greek youth)*
Aladdin's cave	*Aladdin (character in* Arabian Nights*)*
ampere	*A M Ampere (physicist)*
aphrodisiac	*Aphrodite (Greek goddess of love)*
August	*Augustus Caesar (succeeded Julius Caesar)*
bakelite	*Baekeland (inventor)*
Beaufort scale	*Sir F Beaufort (admiral)*
bechamel	*Marquis de Bechamel (courtier)*
begonia	*M Begon (patron of science)*
Benedictine	*Benedictine monks*
Bessemer process	*Sir H Bessemer (engineer)*
Biro	*L Biro (inventor)*
Bismarck herring	*Prince O von Bismarck (statesman)*
Blackwood (bridge)	*E F Blackwood (bridge player)*
bloomers	*Mrs A Bloomer (social reformer)*
bluchers	*G L von Blucher (general)*
bobby	*Sir Robert Peel (statesman)*
bougainvillaea	*L A de Bougainville (navigator)*
bowdlerize	*T Bowdler (expurgator of Shakespeare)*
bowie knife	*J Bowie (American soldier)*
boycott	*Capt C C Boycott (Irish land agent)*
braille	*Louis Braille (teacher)*
Bright's disease	*R Bright (physician)*
brougham	*Lord Brougham*
Bunsen burner	*R W Bunsen (chemist)*

Eponym	Source
Caesarean	*Julius Caesar*
camellia	*J Camellus (Jesuit, botanist)*
cardigan	*Earl of Cardigan (nobleman)*
Casanova	*G J Casanova de Seingalt (adventurer)*
Catherine wheel	*St Catherine (martyr)*
cereal	*Ceres (goddess of agriculture)*
chauvinism	*N Chauvin (Napoleonic veteran)*
chesterfield	*Earl of Chesterfield*
Chicken Tetrazzini	*Louisa Tetrazzini (opera singer)*
Chippendale	*T Chippendale (cabinet maker)*
colt	*S Colt (inventor)*
Colles fracture	*A Colles (surgeon)*
curie	*M Curie (scientist)*
curium	*M & P Curie (scientists)*
dahlia	*A Dahl (botanist)*
Davy lamp	*Sir H Davy (chemist)*
Derby	*Earl of Derby*
derby hat	*Earl of Derby*
derrick	*Derrick (hangman)*
derringer	*H Derringer (inventor)*
diddle	*Jeremy Diddler (character in Raising the Wind)*
diesel	*R Diesel (engineer)*
Disneyesque	*W Disney (cartoonist)*
Dobermann	*L Dobermann (dog breeder)*
doily	*Doiley (linen draper)*
dolomite	*S G de Dolomieu (geologist)*
Dow-Jones index	*C H Dow & E D Jones (economists)*
Draconian	*Draco (legislator)*
Dundreary whiskers	*Lord Dundreary (character in Our American Cousin)*
dunce	*John Duns Scotus (schoolman)*
Eiffel Tower	*Alexandre Eiffel (engineer)*
Electra complex	*Electra (character in Greek tragedy)*
epicure	*Epicurus (philosopher)*
erotic	*Eros (god of love)*
Fahrenheit scale	*G D Fahrenheit (physicist)*
Fallopian tube	*G Fallopius (anatomist)*
fermi	*E Fermi (physicist)*
ferris wheel	*G W G Ferris (engineer)*
Fitzgerald-Lorenz contraction	*G F Fitzgerald (physicist)*
forsythia	*W Forsyth (botanist)*
frangipani	*Frangipani (marquis)*
Friday	*Freia (goddess of beauty)*
fuchsia	*L Fuchs (botanist)*
furphy	*Furphy family (owned foundry)*
Gallup poll	*G H Gallup (statistician)*
galvanize	*L Galvani (physiologist)*
gardenia	*Dr A Garden (naturalist)*
gargantuan	*Gargantua (giant in book Gargantua)*
Geiger counter	*H Geiger (physicist)*
Geissler tube	*H Geissler (mechanic)*
George Cross	*King George VI*
Gladstone bag	*W E Gladstone (statesman)*
Gordian knot	*Gordius (King)*
Graham crackers	*Sylvester Graham (doctor)*
Graves' disease	*R J Graves (physician)*
grevillia	*C F Greville (botanist)*
grog	*Adam Vernon's nickname 'Grogram' (type of coat he wore)*
Gouldian finch	*Elizabeth Gould (wife of John Gould)*
guillotine	*J I Guillotin (physician)*

Eponym	Source	Eponym	Source
Hansard	*L Hansard (printer)*	*Lynch's law*	*Capt W Lynch (soldier)*
Havelock	*General H Havelock*		
Hoover Dam	*President Hoover*	*macadam*	*J L Mc Adam (surveyor)*
Hoover (vacuum cleaner)	*W H Hoover (manufacturer)*	*macadamia*	*J Macadam (chemist)*
		macintosh	*C Macintosh (scientist)*
Jacob's ladder	*Jacob (in Genesis)*	*Magellanic clouds*	*Magellan (explorer)*
Jacquard loom	*J M Jacquard (inventor)*	*magnolia*	*P Magnol (botanist)*
Jaeger	*G Jaeger (scientist)*	*malapropism*	*Mrs Malaprop in* The Rivals
January	*Janus (god of beginnings and endings)*	*mansard roof*	*F Mansard (architect)*
		March	*Mars (the god of war)*
Julian calendar	*Julius Caesar*	*martinet*	*J Martinet (drill master)*
July	*Julius Caesar (born in July)*	*masochist*	*L von Sacher Masoch (novelist)*
June	*Junius (famous Roman family)*	*maudlin*	*Mary Magdalen*
joule	*J P Joule (physicist)*	*mausoleum*	*Mausolus (ancient King)*
		May	*Maiea (goddess of spring)*
Keynesian	*Lord Keynes (economist)*	*Maxim*	*Sir H S Maxim (inventor)*
knickerbocker	*Diedrich Knickerbocker (pretended author of* History of New York*)*	*maxwell*	*J C Maxwell (physicist)*
		Melba sauce	*Dame N Melba (soprano)*
		Melba toast	*Dame N Melba*
lamington	*Baron Lamington*	*Mendelism*	*G J Mendel (botanist)*
Leadbeater's cockatoo	*J Leadbeater (taxidermist)*	*mercerize*	*J Mercer (inventor)*
Leadbeater's possum	*J Leadbeater (taxidermist)*	*mesmerism*	*F A Mesmer (physician)*
Lee-Enfield	*J P Lee (designer), Enfield (where rifle was designed)*	*Mittys*	*Walter Mitty (hero of story by J Thurber)*
leotard	*J Leotard (trapeze performer)*	*Molotov bread basket*	*V M Molotov (statesman)*
Levis	*Levi Strauss (manufacturer)*	*Molotov cocktail*	*V M Molotov (statesman)*
Lewin's honeyeater	*J W Lewin (artist, naturalist)*	*Morris chair*	*W Morris (poet and craftsman)*
Lewis gun	*I N Lewis (soldier)*	*Morse Code*	*S Morse (electrician)*
Listerine	*Lord Lister (father of antiseptic surgery)*		
Lobster Newburg	*Ben Wenburg (First three letters reversed in Wenburg when he fell out with owners of Delmonica's Hotel)*	*namby-pamby*	*Ambrose Phillips (pastoral writer)*
		napoleon	*Napoleon (19th century French emperor)*
		nattier blue	*J M Nattier (painter)*
loganberry	*J H Logan (horticulturalist)*	*newton*	*Sir I Newton (scientist)*
		Newton's laws of motion	*Sir I Newton*

Eponym	Source
nicol prism	W Nicol (scientist, physicist)
nicotine	J Nicot (diplomat)
Nobel prize	Alfred Nobel (inventor)
noisette	P Noisette (rose grower)
Nostradamus	M de Nostredame (astrologer, physician)
Occam's razor	William of Occam (philosopher)
ohm	G S Ohm (physicist)
Ohm's law	G S Ohm
Orwellian	G Orwell (pseudonym of E A Blair)
Otto engine	N A Otto (engineer)
Owenism	Robert Owen (social reformer)
Palladian window	A Palladio (architect)
Pap smear	G N Papanicolaou (devised test)
Parkinson's disease	J Parkinson (surgeon)
Parkinson's law	C N Parkinson (writer)
pascal	B Pascal (scientist)
pasteurization	Louis Pasteur (chemist)
Paterson's curse	Paterson (gardener)
pavlova	A Pavlova (ballerina)
Peach Melba	Dame N Melba (soprano)
peeler	Sir Robert Peel (statesman)
Plimsoll line/mark	S Plimsoll (politician)
poinciana	M de Poinci (governor in W Indies)
poinsettia	J R Poinsett (diplomat)
poise	J L M Poiseuille (physician)
pompadour	Marquise de pompadour (mistress of Louis XV)
Pott's fracture	P Pott (surgeon)
praline	Marshal de Plessis-Praslin
Pulitzer prize	J Pulitzer (newspaper publisher)

Eponym	Source
Pullman car/coach	G M Pullman (designer)
Quixote	Don Quixote (hero of Cervantes' romance)
raglan sleeve	Lord Raglan (commander)
Rhodes Scholar/Scholarships	C J Rhodes (statesman)
Richter Scale	C F Richter (seismologist)
rickettsia	H T Ricketts (pathologist)
rigadoon	Rigaud (dance master)
ritzy	C Ritz (hotel owner)
Rubik's Cube	E Rubik (inventor)
Salk vaccine	J E Salk (scientist)
salmonella	D E Salmon (veterinary surgeon)
sandwich	Earl of Sandwich (nobleman)
Sarich orbital engine	T A Sarich (inventor)
Saturday	Saturn (god of agriculture)
saxhorn	C J & A Sax (instrument makers)
Schick	Col Jacob Schick
sadism	Marquis de Sade (author)
sequoia	Sequoiah (Cherokee)
Sheraton	T Sheraton (furniture maker)
shrapnel	Gen H Shrapnel (inventor)
silhouette	Etienne de Silhouette (author, politician)
spencer	2nd Earl of Spencer (politician)
Spode	J Spode (maker of china)
Stillson pipe, wrench	D C Stillson (inventor)
Stroganoff	P Stroganoff (diplomat)
Teddy bear	Theodore Roosevelt (politician)
Thursday	Thor (god of thunder)
Trotskyism	L Trotsky (politician)

Eponym	Source
Tuesday	*Tiu (god of war)*
Van Allen (radiation) belt	*J A Van Allen (physicist)*
Venn diagram	*J Venn (logician)*
volcano	*Vulcan (Roman god of fire)*
voltaic	*A Volta (physicist)*
watt	*J Watt (engineer)*
weber	*W E Weber (physicist)*
Wedgewood	*J Wedgewood (potter)*
Wednesday	*Woden (god of storms)*
Wendy house	*Wendy (character in* Peter Pan*)*
wellingtons	*Duke of Wellington (general, statesman)*
Winchester rifle	*O F Winchester (manufacturer)*
wistaria	*C Wistar (anatomist)*
Zeppelin	*Count F von Zeppelin (airman)*
zinnia	*J G Zinn (physician, botanist)*

Note: Many cities are also named after people, for example, *Mount Tom Price* after an American, Thomas Moore Price, and *Darwin* after Charles Darwin.

▼ *Words originating from places*

Eponym	Source
antimacassar	*Macassar, Sulawesi*
arras	*Arras, France*
artesian well	*Artois, France*
astrakhan	*Astrakhan, Russia*

Eponym	Source
badminton	*Badminton, England*
Bakewell tart	*Bakewell, Derbyshire*
Balaclava	*Balaclava, Crimea*
bauxite	*Les Baux, France*
bayonet	*Bayonne, France*
Bearnaise sauce	*Bearn, France*
Beaujolais	*Beaujolais, France*
bikini	*Bikini atoll, Marshall Islands*
Bohemian	*Bohemia, Czechoslovakia*
Bordeaux	*Bordeaux, France*
bourbon	*Bourbon County, Kentucky*
Brie	*Brie, France*
Bren (gun)	*Brno (Czech) + Enfield (England)*
Bronx	*Bronx, New York*
Brussels carpet	*Brussels, Belgium*
Brussels lace	*Brussels, Belgium*
Brussels sprouts	*Brussels, Belgium*
calico	*Calicut, India*
calvados	*Calvados, France*
Cambridge blue	*Cambridge, England*
Camembert	*Camembert, France*
canary	*Canary Islands*
cantaloupe	*Cantaluppi, Italy*
Cape Barren goose	*Cape Barren Island, Bass Strait*
Cape Barren tea	*Cape Barren Island, Bass Strait*
cashmere	*Kashmir, India*
Collins Street farmer	*Collins St, Melbourne*
Colorado beetle	*Colorado, US*
Cornish pasty	*Cornwall, England*
champagne	*Champagne, France*
cheviot	*Cheviot Hills, England*
Chianti	*Chianti, Tuscany*
chihuahua	*Chihuahua, Mexico*
Cluny lace	*Cluny, France*

Eponym	Source
Clydesdale	*Clyde, Scotland*
cognac	*Cognac, France*
cologne	*Cologne, Germany*
cretonne	*Creton, Normandy*
damask	*Damascus, Syria*
denim	*Nimes, France*
Devonshire tea	*Devon, England*
Dresden china	*Dresden, Germany*
duffel bag	*Duffel, Belgium*
dumdum bullet	*Dumdum, India*
Dundee cake	*Dundee, Scotland*
Dundee marmalade	*Dundee, Scotland*
Eccles cake	*Eccles, Greater Manchester*
Epsom Handicap	*Epsom, Surrey*
Epsom salts	*Epsom, Surrey*
frankfurt	*Frankfurt, Germany*
gauze	*Gaza, Palestine*
Greenwich mean time	*Greenwich, London*
gruyere	*Gruyere, Switzerland*
hamburger	*Hamburg, Germany*
Havana cigar	*Havana, Cuba*
Hereford	*Hereford, England*
jaffa orange	*Jaffa, Israel*
Jamaica pepper	*Jamaica, W Indies*
jersey	*Jersey, Channel Islands*
jodhpurs	*Jodhpur, India*
lawn	*Laon, France*
lima bean	*Lima, Peru*

Eponym	Source
Limburger	*Limburg, Holland*
limerick	*Limerick, Ireland*
limousine	*Limousin, France*
Lincoln green	*Lincoln, England*
lisle thread	*Lille, France*
Macassar oil	*Macassar, Sulawesi*
Madeira cake	*Madeira, island in Atlantic*
madras	*Madras, India*
magenta	*Battle of Magenta, Italy*
Malacca cane	*Malacca, Malaysia*
manhattan	*Manhattan, New York*
malibu board	*Malibu Beach, California*
manila folder	*Manila, Philippines*
Manila hemp	*Manila, Philippines*
Manila paper	*Manila, Philippines*
Marsala	*Marsala, Sicily*
mayonnaise	*Port Mahon, Minorca*
mazurka	*Mazovia, Poland*
Melton Mowbray pie	*Melton Mowbray, Leics*
meringue	*Mehringen (Germany) or Mehrinyghem*
milliner	*Milan, Italy*
Moreton Bay bug	*Moreton Bay, Queensland*
Moreton Bay chestnut	*Moreton Bay, Queensland*
Moreton Bay fig	*Moreton Bay, Queensland*
moselle	*Moselle, Germany*
Murray cod	*Murray River, Australia*
Murrumbidgee jam	*Murrumbidgee River, Australia*
Neapolitan	*Naples, Italy*
Newmarket	*Newmarket, Cambridgeshire*
Olympic	*Olympia, Greece*
Oslo lunch	*Oslo, Norway*

Eponym	Source
Paisley	*Paisley, Scotland*
Panama hat	*Panama, Central America*
Parmesan cheese	*Parma, Italy*
Parramatta grass	*Parramatta, NSW*
Patna rice	*Patna, India*
Perrier	*Perrier spring, Vergeze, France*
Persian carpets	*Persia*
Piccadilly bushman	*Picadilly, London*
Pilsener	*Pilsen, Czechoslovakia*
Polwarth	*Polwarth, Victoria (Aust)*
plaster of Paris	*Paris, France*
Portland cement	*Isle of Portland, Dorset*
Rambouillet	*Rambouillet, France*
Rhinestone	*Rhine, Germany*
Rhine Riesling	*Rhine, Germany*
Roquefort	*Roquefort, France*
Rottweiler	*Rottweil, Germany*
sardine	*Sardinia*
Satsuma ware	*Satsuma, Japan*
Sauterne	*Sauternes, France*
saxony	*Saxony, Germany*
Sealyham terrier	*Sealyham, Wales*
Seville orange	*Seville, Spain*
Sevres porcelain	*Sevres, France*
shanghai	*Shanghai, China*
Shetland lace	*Shetland Islands*
Shetland pony	*Shetland Islands*
Shetland wool	*Shetland Islands*
Siamese cat	*Siam*
Siamese twins	*Siam*
spaniel	*Spain*
Stilton	*Stilton, Cambridgeshire*
Stockholm pitch/tar	*Stockholm, Sweden*

Eponym	Source
Sussex spaniel	*Sussex, England*
tabasco	*Tabasco, Mexico*
tangerine	*Tangier, Morocco*
tobacco	*Tabago, Antilles*
Tokay	*Tokaj, Hungary*
Toledo	*Toledo, Spain*
tulle	*Tulle, France*
tuxedo	*Tuxedo Park, New York City*
Vichy water	*Vichy, France*
Waterford glass	*Waterford, Ireland*
Waterloo	*Waterloo, Belgium*
Westminster system	*Westminster, London*
wiener	*Vienna*
Wimmera shower	*Wimmera, Victoria*
Windsor chair	*Windsor, Berkshire*
Windsor soap	*Windsor, Berkshire*
Worcester sauce	*Worcester, England*
worsted	*Worste (d), Norfolk*
York gum	*York, W Australia*
Yorkshire pudding	*Yorkshire, England*

▼ *Words originating from institutions*

Eponym	Source
Eggs Benedict	*Benedict's Restaurant, New York*
Port Salut	*Trappist Abbey, France*
Tattersalls	*Tattersall's Hotel, Sydney*

Points to think about

Points to consider when students are learning about eponyms include:

▼ *Introducing eponyms*

Once students have a body of words they recognize and they are starting to think about the meaning relationships between words, or are capable of thinking about these relationships, it is appropriate to introduce eponyms.

▼ *Eponyms are words derived from a variety of names*

Explain to students that eponyms are words that originate from a variety of names — the names of people, places or institutions, and that the introduction of eponyms is one way words become part of the English language.

▼ *Knowing where the word originates from helps with its spelling*

Talk with the students about how knowing where an eponym originates from helps with its spelling, for example, *pasteurization* is spelt the same way as the person from whom it originated, Louis *Pasteur*, and therefore it is not spelt *pasturization*.

▼ *Confirming the derivation of eponyms in dictionaries*

Encourage students to note the way some dictionaries indicate the origin of eponyms.

Activities

The following activities can be used to help students learn about eponyms:

▼ *Creating a fascination with words*

An important reason for teaching about eponyms is to create a fascination with the English language. When students use eponyms in their writing talk with them about the origins of the eponyms and encourage them to confirm these in a dictionary.

▼ *Developing a class list*

As the students discover eponyms when reading and writing assist them to develop a class list and encourage them to add to the list as they find other eponyms. When listing eponyms ensure the students understand their meanings and that they are words they are likely to use in their writing. It would be useful to indicate on the class list the origin of the eponym, whether it be a person's name, a place or an institution.

Talk with the students about where they can find such information, and ask them to think about how knowing about eponyms and the meaning relationship that exists between an eponym and its origin can assist them with their writing.

▼ *Publishing a class book*

As the class list develops assist the students to publish a book of eponyms, and ask them to classify the eponyms into groups according to their origins. Involve the students in deciding on the organization of the book, for example, the eponyms could be arranged according to their origin or alphabetically. The book could have a contents page to make it easy to refer to. It can be placed in the class library for the students to refer to or borrow.

▼ *Playing games with eponyms*

It may become apparent during discussions with students or from reading their writing that further clarification of their understandings about eponyms is necessary. If this is so, students could play some of the games in Chapter 11 using eponyms. The words selected for the games should be taken from class lists, students' writing and reading materials, lists of words they have selected to learn, topic lists, and other sources that are relevant to them.

12 Waterproof material patented by the inventor C. Macintosh.
13 Buttered bread with filling. Named after the 4th Earl of Sandwich.

Down
10 Plant with brilliantly colored foliage. Named after M. Begon.

Resources

Beeching, Cyril Leslie, *A Dictionary of Eponyms*, Oxford University Press, New York, 1988.

Proprietary words

A proprietary word is a proprietary name or trade mark. The list below is provided as a resource of the range of proprietary words and it is not intended as a list of words to be learned.

Amytal	*Airwick*
Aqualung	*Band-aid*
Benzedrine	*Biro*
Carborundum	*BriNylon*
Brylcreem	*Can-o-Mat*
Caterpillar	*Cellophane*
Chubb	*Coca-Cola/Coke*
Cointreau	*Colt*
Corona	*Dictaphone*
Dictograph	*Dixie*
Duco	*Elastoplast*
Esky	*Formica*
Frigidaire	*Frisbee*
Gillette	*Hoover*
Jacuzzi	*Jaeger*
Klaxon	*Kewpie*
Kleenex	*Kodak*
Laminex	*Land Rover*
Laundromat	*Levis*

Across
3 Puzzle consisting of cubes. Named after inventor, E. Rubik.
6 An annual prize awarded from bequest of Alfred Nobel.
8 Method used to partially sterilize milk. Named after Louis Pasteur.
9 High class, luxurious. Named after owner of luxury hotels, C. Ritz.
11 Vaccine developed against poliomyelitis. Named after J.E. Salk.

Down
1 Line on ship's side, named after S. Plimsoll, an English M.P.
2 A meringue dessert named after a Russian ballerina, A. Pavlova.
4 Ballpoint pen, named after Hungarian inventor, L. Biro.
5 Bacteria named after veterinary surgeon, D. E. Salmon.
7 Thin crisp toast named after Australian soprano Dame Nellie Melba.

Listerine
Masonite
Mixmaster
Nichrome
Ouija-board
Perspex
Ping-Pong
Polaroid
Pyrex
Schick
Spam
Tabasco
Technicolor
Terylene
Vaseline
Wimpy
Yale
Xerox

Martini
Methedrine
Monotype
Orlon
Perrier
Pianola
Plasticine
Primus
Roneo
Sellotape
Stubbies
Tarmac
Teletype
Thermos
Vegemite
Windcheater
Yo-Yo

Points to think about

▼ *Introducing proprietary words*

Once students have a body of words they recognize and they are starting to think about, or are capable of thinking about the origins of proprietary words, it is appropriate to introduce them.

▼ *Proprietary words should begin with capital letters*

Many proprietary terms, including trademarks and brand names, have become everyday household words. Although they are often written in lower case it is incorrect to do so — they should begin with a capital letter to reflect their origins. The Australian *Style Manual for Authors, Editors and Printers* (see Resources, page 123) warns publishers against using proprietary words and suggests that publishers insist on these words being printed with

capital letters to avoid possible litigation. Relate this to students' use of proprietary words in their personal writing.

▼ *Introducing words into the English language*

The English language is a living language and new words are constantly being introduced. The creation of proprietary terms is one way new words enter the language.

Activities

The following activities can be used to help students learn about proprietary words:

▼ *Developing a class list*

When students discover proprietary words in their reading talk with them about the proprietary words they know and write these on a class list. When listing proprietary words ensure the students understand their meanings and that they are words they are likely to use in their writing. It may be useful to indicate the source of the proprietary word, for example, a billboard, magazine, and so on. Encourage students to add to the class chart as they find other proprietary words, and to note whether the words were spelled with a capital letter. Ask the students to think about how knowing about proprietary words will assist them in their writing.

▼ *Using published materials as models for students' writing*

Use advertisements and other texts to demonstrate to students the spelling and use of proprietary words. Ask the students to collect advertisements and note the spelling of proprietary words and other words that differ from the conventional spelling, such as *nite* for *night*. Discuss the reason for this (for example, attention grabbing) and the use of poetic licence when spelling some words in advertisements. Relate this to the students' personal writing, informing them that the only time such licence would be available to them as writers would be if they were writing advertisements.

▼ *Publishing a class book*

Assist the students to publish a book of proprietary terms, including in it a comment about the need for proprietary terms to begin with a capital letter. Place the book in the class library for the students to refer to or borrow.

Resources

Commonwealth of Australia, *Style Manual for Authors, Editors and Printers,* (4th Edition), Australian Government Publishing Service, Canberra, 1986.

Shortened Words

8

Abbreviations

A shortened word can be a contraction or an abbreviation. (For information on Contractions refer to pages 128 to 131.) An abbreviation is an abbreviated form of another word. A word is often shortened when some of the letters at the end of the word are left out and not replaced with an apostrophe, for example, *cafe* for *cafeteria*. However, other words are shortened when the letters at the beginning of a word are left out and not replaced with an apostrophe, for example, *burger* for *hamburger*. Some shortened words are quite different from their longer form, for example, *crisp* for *potato chip*.

Below is a list of common abbreviations. This list is provided as a resource of the range of shortened words and it is not intended as a list of words to be learned.

ad	*advertisement*
admin	*administration*
aggro	*aggravation, aggression*
ammo	*ammunition*
amp	*ampere*
anon	*anonymous*
appro	*approval*
bag	*baggage*
bicarb	*bicarbonate of soda*
bra	*brassiere*

burger	*hamburger*
bus	*omnibus*
cab	*taxi cab*
cab	*cabriolet*
cafe	*cafeteria*
cello	*violincello*
champ	*champion*
co-ed	*co-educational*
Coke	*Coca-Cola*
compo	*compensation*
confab	*confabulation*
cox	*coxswain*
crisp	*potato chip*
crit	*criticism*
croc	*crocodile*
curio	*curiosity*
deb	*debutante*
demo	*demonstration*
dero	*derelict*
disco	*discotheque*
doc	*doctor*
dorm	*dormitory*

exam	*examination*		*mod*	*modern*
			mono	*monophonic*
fax	*facsimile*		*morn*	*morning*
feds	*Federal official*		*muso*	*musician*
flu	*influenza*			
fluoro	*fluorescent*		*panto*	*pantomime*
fridge	*refrigerator*		*para*	*paratroops*
			perk	*percolate*
gents	*gentlemen*		*perm*	*permanent wave*
gym	*gymnasium*		*perv*	*pervert*
gyno	*gynaecologist*		*petrol*	*petroleum*
gyro	*gyroscope*		*phone*	*telephone*
			photo	*photograph*
helio	*heliograph*		*phys ed*	*physical education*
hippo	*hippopotamus*		*physio*	*physiotherapist*
			piano	*pianoforte*
info	*information*		*plane*	*aeroplane*
inter	*intermediate*		*pleb*	*plebeian*
intercom	*intercommunication*		*polio*	*poliomyelitis*
intro	*introduction*		*pop*	*popular music*
			porno	*pornography*
Jag	*Jaguar*		*prac*	*practical*
			pram	*perambulator*
kilo	*kilogram*		*prefab*	*prefabricated*
			prelims	*preliminaries*
lab	*laboratory*		*prem*	*premature*
lit	*literature*		*prep*	*preparation*
log	*logarithm*		*pressie*	*present*
logo	*logotype*		*pro*	*professional*
lube	*lubricate*		*prof*	*professor*
			prom	*promenade*
maths	*mathematics*		*prop*	*proprietor/propeller/property*
memo	*memorandum*		*pub*	*public house*
metho	*methylated spirits*		*pud*	*pudding*
mike	*microphone*		*pusher*	*push chair*
min	*minute*			

rad	*radical*
recap	*recapitulation*
ref	*referee*
rehab	*rehabilitate*
rep	*representative, repertory*
Repat	*Repatriation*
repro	*reproduction*
revs	*revolutions*
rhino	*rhinoceros*
Salvo	*Salvation Army person*
sax	*saxophone*
schizo	*schizophrenic*
scrum	*scrummage*
speedo	*speedometer*
stereo	*stereophonic, stereotype, stereographic*
tacho	*tachometer*
talc	*talcum powder*
Tarmac	*tarmacadam*
taxi	*taximeter cab*
Tatts	*Tattersalls*
tech	*technical*
temp	*temporary*
tramp	*trampoline*
turps	*turpentine*
tux	*tuxedo*
typo	*typographical error*
ump	*umpire*
uni	*university*
van	*vanguard*
vet	*veterinarian*
vocab	*vocabulary*

wellies	*Wellington boots*
Xmas	*Christmas*
zoo	*zoological gardens*

Points to think about

Points to consider when students are learning about abbreviations include:

▼ *Introducing abbreviations*

Once students have a body of words they recognize and they are starting to think about the meaning relationships between words, or are capable of thinking about these relationships, it is appropriate to introduce abbreviations.

▼ *Comparing abbreviations with contractions*

Abbreviations consist of the initial letter and other letters in the word, but they do not usually consist of the initial and the final letters of the original word. Shortened words that consist of the first and the last letters of the original word are contractions, for example *Dr* (**D**octo**r**) and *Dept* (**Dep**artmen**t**). For more information about contractions see page 128.

▼ *Some abbreviations do not have full stops*

Explain to the students that due to common usage many abbreviations have become words in their own right and do not need full stops. For example, *vet* does not need a full stop.

▼ *Introducing new words into the English language*

The forming of abbreviations is one way words are introduced to the English language, for example, *rad* for the word *radical*.

▼ *Confirming the origin of abbreviations in dictionaries*

Encourage students to confirm the spellings of the full form of abbreviations in a dictionary and talk with them about the way some dictionaries indicate which words are abbreviations.

▼ *The appropriate use of abbreviations in writing*

Talk with the students about when it is appropriate to use abbreviations in their personal writing. For example, it may not be appropriate to use them in a piece of narrative.

Activities

The following activities can be used to help students learn about abbreviations:

▼ *Developing a class list*

As the students discover abbreviations when reading or when they begin using them in their writing start a class list of abbreviations and encourage the students to add to the list as they find others. When listing abbreviations ensure the students understand their meanings and that they are words they are likely to use in their writing. Talk with the students about the ways words may be shortened, ensuring that they understand the difference between an abbreviation and a contraction.

Using words from the class list demonstrate to the students how the abbreviations are related in meaning to the words from which they originate, for example *disco* and <u>disco</u>*theque*. It may be useful to underline the abbreviation within the full form of the word, as shown in the previous example.

As students find other abbreviations in their reading and writing add these and the words from which they originated to the charts.

▼ *Students selecting words to learn*

Some of the words students select to learn may be abbreviations, for example, *physio*. It is useful to also list the word from which it originated, *physiotherapist,* and other meaning related words such as *physiotherapists* and *physiotherapy* to highlight the meaning relationship between them. Talk with the students about how listing the full form of the abbreviation and other related words will help them with their writing.

▼ *Students complete activities with shortened words*

It may become apparent during discussions with students or from reading their writing that further clarification of the meaning relationship that exists between abbreviations and the words from which they originate is necessary. If this is so, students could complete activities similar to the following and could also create such activities for their peers to complete. The words selected for the activities should be taken from class lists, students' writing and reading materials, lists of words they have selected to learn, topic lists, and other sources that are relevant to them.

1 This activity focuses on the meaning relationships that exist between abbreviations and the words from which they originate. Students are given words written in their abbreviated form and asked to write the words from which they originated. For example:

Here are some abbreviations:
maths math (U.S.A.) ....
gym ....
phys ed. ....
mike ....
exam ....
hippo ....
flu ....
Write the full form of these abbreviations.

2 Many games may be played using abbreviations and the words from which they originate, for example, crosswords.

Across

5 Vet
7 Burger
8 Fridge
9 Cafe
11 Disco
12 Petrol
13 Physio

Down

1 Lab
2 Photo
3 Demo
4 Intro
6 Ump
10 Phone

Refer to Chapter 11 for other suitable games.

Contractions

There are two types of contractions.

One type of contraction is the word *it's*, where two words are joined, and letters are left out between the two words *it* and *is*. An apostrophe is inserted between the two words where the letters have been omitted.

The second type of contraction is the shortened form of a word that ends in the same letter as the word itself, for example, *Mr* for *Mister* and *Dr* for *Doctor*. In Australia, such contractions do not require full stops, however, in the United States a full stop is required, for example, Mr. and Dr.

Below is a list of common contractions of the first type, where an apostrophe is used to indicate that letters have been omitted. This list is provided as a resource of the range of contractions and it is not intended as a list of words to be learned.

Contractions with *is* or *has*		**Contractions with *not***	
he is/has	*he's*	could not	*couldn't*
she is/has	*she's*	would not	*wouldn't*
it is/has	*it's*	should not	*shouldn't*
that is/has	*that's*	did not	*didn't*
there is/has	*there's*	do not	*don't*
how is/has	*how's*	has not	*hasn't*
where is/has	*where's*	had not	*hadn't*
what is/has	*what's*	have not	*haven't*
here is	*here's*	was not	*wasn't*
		were not	*weren't*
		will not	*won't*
		does not	*doesn't*
		is not	*isn't*
		are not	*aren't*
		can not	*can't*

Contractions with *have*		**Contractions with** *had* or *would*	
I have	*I've*	*I had*	*I'd*
you have	*you've*	*you had*	*you'd*
we have	*we've*	*they had*	*they'd*
they have	*they've*	*he had*	*he'd*
		she had	*she'd*
		we had	*we'd*

Contractions with *are*		**Contractions with** *will*	
we are	*we're*	*we will*	*we'll*
you are	*you're*	*you will*	*you'll*
they are	*they're*	*they will*	*they'll*
		he will	*he'll*
		she will	*she'll*
		I will	*I'll*

Contraction with *am*	
I am	*I'm*

Points to think about

Points to consider when students are learning about contractions with apostrophes include:

▼ *Introducing contractions*

Once students have a body of words they recognize and they are starting to think about the meaning relationships between words, or are capable of thinking about these relationships, it is appropriate to introduce contractions.

▼ *The meaning and spelling of a contraction*

The meaning of a contraction is the same as the meaning of the two original words from which it is formed. Knowing the origin of a contraction can help students learn its spelling.

▼ *Changes that occur to the spelling of words from which a contraction is derived, when contractions are formed*

When a contraction is formed the number of letters omitted varies. For example:

they're	they **a**re (one letter)
they've	they **ha**ve (two letters)
they'd	they **woul**d (four letters)

▼ *The consistent changes that occur to the spelling of words when contractions are formed*

When a contraction is formed the same letters are omitted from the second word of the contraction each time. For example, the letter *a* from *are* (we're, they're, you're . . .), *o* from *not* (don't, can't, won't, isn't . . .), and so on. Consequently the apostrophe is always positioned in the same place for all contractions formed with the word *are* or the word *not*. If students know how to spell *are* or *not*, and so on, in one contraction, it will help them to spell them and know where to place the apostrophe in other contractions. Ask the students to think about how this will assist them in their writing.

▼ *Teaching about contractions that are relevant to students' writing needs*

There is no particular sequence in which contractions should be studied. Those students require for their personal writing needs are the contractions that should be dealt with at any given time. It may be that a contraction is studied on more than one occasion in a particular year level, and it may be that the same contraction is also studied again in subsequent years, depending on the writing needs of the students.

Activities

The following activities can be used to help students learn about contractions:

▼ *Developing a class list*

As students discover contractions in their reading and writing assist them to develop a class list and encourage them to add to the list as they find other contractions. When listing contractions ensure the students understand their meanings and that they are words they are likely to use in their writing. It would be useful to include on the list the contractions and the words from which they are formed. For example:

don't   do not
he'll   he will

Continue to demonstrate to students the meaning relationship that exists between contractions and the words from which they are formed and ask them to think about how knowing this will assist them with their writing.

Don't do not let's let us. She's She is
I've I have
They'll they will you're you are
I'll I will
we'll we will
I'm I am
It's It is
we're we are
that's that is
where's where is
didn't did not

A copy of a class list of contractions, with words from which they originate. A child wrote out the list. It was photocopied and given to each child in class as a record of the class spelling activity.

▼ *Classifying contractions*

When the students have listed a reasonable number of contractions assist them to sort the contractions according to the words from which they are formed, for example, all contractions derived from words containing *not* or *is* would be grouped together respectively. Make a class list for each group of contractions and encourage students to add to these lists as they discover contractions in their reading and writing. Talk with the students about how knowing the way contractions are formed will assist them when they are attempting to spell contractions in their writing.

▼ *Publishing a class book*

Assist the students to publish a class book of contractions. This could consist of the collated class charts or it may be a separate publication. Involve the students in deciding on the organization of the big book. The book could have a contents page to make it easy to refer to and the students may like to include a page where each of them writes something that they have learned about contractions and how this knowledge helps them with their writing. The big book should be placed in the class library for the students to refer to or borrow.

▼ *Students complete activities with contractions*

To clarify students' understandings about contractions activities similar to the following may be completed. The words selected could be taken from words students have selected to learn, class lists, their personal writing or reading materials.

1 Students write the two words that are combined to form the contractions derived from the word *not* and one other word. They may like to refer to a dictionary or wordbook to confirm their spelling attempts. For example:

Rewrite the contractions in their expanded form and in each case underline the letter that has been replaced by the apostrophe.				
couldn't	=	could	+	....
hasn't	=	has	+	....
isn't	=	....	+	not
wouldn't	=	....	+	....
shouldn't	=	....	+	....
haven't	=	....	+	....

Continue to demonstrate to students the meaning relationship that exists between contractions and the words from which they are formed. Ask the students to think about how knowing what happens to the word *not* in contractions will assist them in their writing.

It may be useful to repeat this activity with contractions derived from other words, such as *will, would, have* and *are.*

2 Students write the contractions derived from the word *is* and one other word. They may like to refer to a dictionary or wordbook to confirm their spelling attempts. For example:

Write the contractions for these words:		
that is	=	....
he is	=	....
she is	=	....
here is	=	....
there is	=	....
where is	=	....

Continue to demonstrate to students the meaning relationship that exists between contractions and the words from which they are formed. Ask the students to think about how knowing what happens to the word *is* in contractions will assist them in their writing.

It may benefit the students to repeat this activity with contractions derived from other words, such as *will, would, have* and *are.*

▼ *Students selecting words to learn*

Some of the words students select to learn may be contractions, for example, *didn't.* It is useful to list other contractions that are derived from the same word *(not)* for students to learn, for example, *wouldn't, doesn't* and *wasn't.* Ask the students to think about how this will help them with their writing.

The Possessive Apostrophe

9

Apostrophes are used in contractions and to indicate possession.

In contractions apostrophes indicate that one or more letters have been left out (refer to pages 128 to 131).

To show that something is owned by or belongs to someone or something, the possessive apostrophe is used. For example:

the astronaut's suit — the suit that belongs to the astronaut
the spider's eye — the eye that belongs to the spider

Below are examples of the common use of the possessive apostrophe.

1 Singular nouns that do not end in *s*
For singular nouns that end in any letter other than *s* the possessive is formed by adding *'s*:

the magician's wand
John's book
today's weather

2 Singular nouns that end in *s*
For singular nouns that end in *s* the possessive is formed by adding *'s*:

Burns's poems
Dickens's novels

3 Plural nouns that do not end in *s*
For plural nouns that end in any letter other than *s* the possessive is formed by adding *'s*:

the mice's food
the people's army

4 Plural nouns that end in *s*
For plural nouns that end in *s* the possessive is formed by adding an apostrophe after the *s*:

the parents' meeting
the Smiths' home
my brothers' wives
the ladies' coats

5 Plural nouns ending in *en*
For plural nouns that end in *en* the possessive is formed by adding *'s*:

the children's party
the men's books
the women's letters

Points to think about

Points to consider when students are learning about the possessive apostrophe include:

▼ *Introducing the possessive apostrophe*

Once students have a body of words they recognize and they are starting to notice the use of apostrophes in words it is appropriate to introduce the possessive apostrophe.

▼ *Generally the possessive apostrophe is only used with nouns*

The apostrophe is only used with nouns and not with the pronouns *hers, his, theirs, yours, ours* and *its*, because these already indicate possession. (**Note:** *it's* is a contraction meaning *it is*.) Note, however, that the apostrophe is used in *one's, someone's, everybody's* and *nobody's*.

▼ *Joint ownership and the possessive apostrophe*

Where there is joint ownership of something the apostrophe *s* should be added to the last word only, for example:

Debbie and Richard's car

If the ownership is not joint, each name has the possessive apostrophe, for example:

Debbie's and Richard's cars

▼ *The possessive apostrophe and time*

When expressing time, the apostrophe is increasingly omitted from the plural forms of words, for example:

ten minutes delay
twelve months notice

However, this is not so for the singular forms of words when expressing time, for example:

a minute's delay
a month's notice

▼ *The possessive apostrophe and place names*

Place names tend to be spelled without the possessive apostrophe, for example:

St Leonards
Batemans Bay

▼ *The possessive apostrophe where nouns are being used as adjectives*

When words such as *teachers* or *writers* are being used as adjectives and not as nouns, for example, the *Teachers Union* or the *Writers Society* the possessive apostrophe is not used.

Activities

The following activities can be used to help students learn about the possessive apostrophe:

▼ *Developing a class list*

As students begin noticing the use of apostrophes in their reading materials begin a class list of these words. Initially the students will not realize the difference between apostrophes being used in contractions or to indicate possession. It is important to continue using literature to model the way writers use apostrophes. To assist students to learn about the different functions of apostrophes group the words, initially according to those where the apostrophes are replacing a letter or group of letters in contractions, and those where the apostrophe is not replacing letters.

Assist the students to discover what the function of the apostrophe is where it is not replacing letters, that is, the possessive apostrophe. Again, use literature to model the use of the possessive apostrophe as well as situations the students experience in daily classroom life, for example, *the teacher's pen*, *the girls' toilets*, *Shelley's birthday*, and so on. List such examples on class charts for the students to refer to when writing. It is likely that this process may need to happen for several years before all students understand how to use the possessive apostrophe.

Talk with the students about who or what possesses something, ensuring that they understand the function of the possessive apostrophe. It may be helpful to also write the words with the possessive apostrophe in another form. For example:

> the teacher's pen — the pen that belonged to the teacher
> the girls' toilets — the toilets that belong to the girls
> Shelley's birthday — the birthday that belongs to Shelley

When writing in her diary this Year 1 student demonstrates some understanding of the use of the possessive apostrophe.

Ask students to note whether the noun was singular or plural, whether or not the noun ended in the letter *s* and where the apostrophe was positioned — before or after the final *s*. Ask them to write their theories about why the possessive apostrophe is placed before or after the final *s* in a word. It may be useful to date these generalizations. Encourage the students to add to the list of words that demonstrate the use of the possessive apostrophe as they find other examples in their reading and writing and assist them to review and refine their theories about its use.

▼ *Using literature as a model for students' writing*

Continue to use examples of literature to demonstrate to students how authors use the possessive apostrophe and ask them to think about how knowing this will assist them in their own writing.

▼ *Classifying words that contain the possessive apostrophe and thinking about its position in words*

As the class list of words that demonstrate the use of the possessive apostrophe develops, assist students to sort the words into various groups, for example, words that are singular, plural, end in *s* and do not end in *s*. Begin separate class charts for each group of words with the possessive apostrophe and assist the students to write statements that explain the use of such in each instance. Display these lists in the classroom for the students to refer to. It may be useful for them to add another page on which they list questions they can ask themselves when determining where to place the possessive apostrophe. For example:

Some students may want individual copies of the questions to place in their writing folders.

Encourage the students to add to the lists as they find other examples of the use of the possessive apostrophe, and assist them to review and refine their theories. Talk with the students about how knowing about the possessive apostrophe will assist them when writing.

▼ *Students search for examples of the possessive apostrophe and compare its use with singular and plural words*

Students could be asked to search their reading materials and current pieces of writing for words with the possessive apostrophe. They may then produce a chart to demonstrate what they have learned about the use of the possessive apostrophe, for example, a chart that contrasts the singular and various plural forms of words and their possessive case.

> the boy's lollies (only one boy)
> the boys' lollies (more than one boy)
> the child's toy (only one child)
> the children's toy (more than one child)
> the witch's hat (only one witch)
> the witches' hats (more than one witch)
> the elf's cap (only one elf)
> the elves' caps (more than one elf)
> the baby's cot (only one baby)
> the babies' cots (more than one baby)
> the mouse's hole (only one mouse)
> the mice's hole (more than one mouse)

The charts could be displayed for students to refer to when writing or they could be made into a book and placed in the class library for the students to refer to and borrow.

Resources

Commonwealth of Australia, *Style Manual for Authors, Editors and Printers,* (4th Edition), Australian Government Publishing Service, 1986.

Alternative Spellings

10

Sometimes there is more than one way to spell a word in English. At times there is more than one acceptable spelling in British English, for example, *cipher/cypher* and *focusing/focussing* and at times one of the alternative spellings may be the American English spelling, for example, *theater/theatre*.

Below are some examples of alternative spellings. This list is provided as a resource of the range of alternative spellings and it is not intended as a list of words to be learned.

Case 1: ae/e

British English	American English	Australian Usage
mediaeval	*medieval*	*Either is acceptable.*
encyclopaedia	*encyclopedia*	*Either is acceptable.*
primaeval	*primeval*	*Either is acceptable.*
leukaemia	*leukemia*	*Either is acceptable.*
orthopaedic	*orthopedic*	*orthopaedic*
paediatric	*pediatric*	*paediatric*
aesthetics	*esthetics*	*aesthetics*

Note: The *ae* spelling is still used for words such as *paediatrician* and *aesthetics*. The use of *e* rather than *ae* is now standard American usage and is creeping into Australian usage.

Case 2: oe/e

British English	American English	Australian Usage
oesophagus	*esophagus*	*Either is acceptable.*
oestrogen	*estrogen*	*oestrogen*
manoeuvre	*maneuvre*	*manoeuvre*
foetus	*fetus*	*foetus*
amoeba	*ameba*	*amoeba*
diarrhoea	*diarrhea*	*Either is acceptable.*

Note: There is a move towards *e* rather than *oe* in Australian usage. The *oe* has virtually disappeared from the words *(o)ecology, (o)economics* and *(o)ecumenical*. However, it does not seem likely that the spelling of *Oedipus* will change.

Case 3: er/re

British English	American English	Australian Usage
litre	*liter*	*litre*
kilolitre	*kiloliter*	*kilolitre*
centre	*center*	*centre*
kilometre	*kilometer*	*kilometre*

British English	American English	Australian Usage
theatre	*theater*	*theatre*
fibre	*fiber*	*fibre*
meagre	*meager*	*meagre*
sombre	*somber*	*sombre*
spectre	*specter*	*spectre*
louvre	*louver*	*Either is acceptable.*
sabre	*saber*	*sabre*
calibre	*caliber*	*calibre*
lustre	*luster*	*lustre*
sepulchre	*sepulcher*	*sepulchre*

Case 4: or/our

British English	American English	Australian Usage
colour	*color*	*Either is acceptable.*
rumour	*rumor*	*Either is acceptable.*
favour	*favor*	*Either is acceptable.*
vigour	*vigor*	*Either is acceptable.*
vapour	*vapor*	*Either is acceptable.*
armour	*armor*	*Either is acceptable.*

Note: In mid-1985 six of the eleven major newspapers in Australia used the *or* spelling. For example, readers of The *Age* and *Adelaide Courier* encounter *or* spellings every day. Consequently, they can no longer be called American spellings.

A number of words have already undergone a spelling change, for example, from *terro(u)r* to *terror, governo(u)r* to *governor* and *erro(u)r* to *error.*

Some words that end in *our* are not pronounced in the same way as the *our* words listed above. These words retain the ending *our,* for example, *devour, pour* and *contour.*

Some words spelled with *our* drop the *u* before adding various suffixes, for example, *honour* but *honorary, humour* but *humorous* and *odour* but *odorless.* If the *or* spelling is used many of the existing complications, for example *honour, honorary* and *honourable,* will disappear.

Case 5: m/mme

British English	American English	Australian Usage
kilogram/me	*kilogram*	*kilogram*
program/me	*program*	*Either is acceptable.*
gram/me	*gram*	*gram*

Note: *Program* is the only acceptable spelling when referring to a computer program.

Case 6: l/ll

British English	American English	Australian Usage
chiselling	*chiseling*	*chiselling*
rebelling	*rebelling*	*rebelling*
revelling	*reveling*	*revelling*
quarelling	*quareling*	*quarelling*
levelling	*leveling*	*levelling*

Note: In British English the final *l* in a word of two or more syllables is doubled before adding the suffixes *ing* and *ed,* regardless of whether or not the final syllable is stressed. For example, *level* and *rebel* become *levelling* and *rebelling.* However, in American English the difference in stress is indicated. Where the stress is on the final syllable of the original word the final *l* is doubled, for example, *rebe'lling,* but when the final syllable is not stressed the final *l* is not doubled, for example, *le'veling.* (' denotes stressed vowel in stressed syllable.)

Case 7: ize/ise

British English	American English	Australian Usage
sympathise/ize	*sympathize*	*Either is acceptable.*
harmonise/ize	*harmonize*	*Either is acceptable.*
Pasteurise/ize	*Pasteurize*	*Either is acceptable.*

Many words may be spelled with the *ize* or *ise* ending. However, some words must be spelled with *ise* and not *ize* for example, *supervise, televise, chastise, despise,* and so on. Alternately, where a word is both a noun and a verb, the verb cannot be spelled with *ise*, for example *prize, size* and *capsize*.

Because more words must take the *ise* ending than must take the *ize* ending, it is often considered easier to opt for the *ise* ending in Australia. The *ise* ending is used by Australian newspapers and government offices. However, in America, the *ize* ending is becoming standard.

Other examples of alternative spellings

British English	American English	Australian Usage
practise (verb)	*practice (verb)*	*practise (verb)*
practice (noun)	*practice (noun)*	*practice (noun)*
blonde	*blond*	*Either is acceptable.*
busing	*bussing*	*Either is acceptable.*
kerb	*curb*	*Either is acceptable.*
disc/disk	*disk*	*Either is acceptable.*
gaol/jail	*jail*	*Either is acceptable.*
pedlar	*peddler/pedler*	*pedlar*
veranda/verandah	*veranda/verandah*	*Either is acceptable.*
Scotch whisky	*whiskey*	*whisky*
Irish and American		
whiskey	*whiskey*	*whisky*
calicoes	*calicos*	*Either is acceptable.*

Note: Blond is now starting to be used in the Australian press.

Points to think about

Points to consider when students are learning about alternative spellings include:

▼ *Introducing alternative spellings*

There is no point in dealing with alternative spellings for words until students have a body of words they recognize and show in their writing an awareness of alternative spellings for words or they notice them when reading.

▼ *Using alternative spelling patterns consistently*

In countries like Australia where an alternative spelling is acceptable, it is important to consistently opt for the one spelling pattern in a piece of writing, for example, *ize* and not *ise*. As well as doing so for words from the same word family, for example, *recognize, recognized, recognizable, recognizes,* and so on, other words where the alternative spelling can be used should also be spelled with *ize,* not *ise*.

▼ *Confirming alternative spellings*

Students should be encouraged to check or confirm spellings of words in dictionaries or wordbooks to see if an alternative spelling is an option. It is important that they note which country the book was published in.

▼ *Teaching about alternative spelling patterns that are relevant to students' writing needs*

There is no particular sequence in which alternative spelling patterns should be studied. Those students require for their personal writing needs are the alternative spelling patterns that should be dealt with at any given time. It may be that an alternative spelling pattern is studied on more than one occasion in a particular year level, and it may be that the same alternative spelling pattern is also studied again in subsequent years, depending on the writing needs of the students. If an alternative spelling pattern is studied on more than one occasion it is likely that the words being considered will be different words.

Activities

The following activities can be used to help students learn about alternative spellings:

▼ *Using literature as a model for students' writing*

Use examples of literature to demonstrate to the students an author's use of consistent spelling patterns and relate this to their need to use consistent spelling patterns in their own writing.

▼ *Developing a class list*

As the students discover alternative spellings when reading begin a class list for each alternative spelling identified, for example *or/our, ize/ise* and *m/mme*. When listing words with alternative spellings ensure the students understand their meanings and that they are words they are likely to use in their writing. Ask the students to note where the piece of writing was published and which spelling pattern was used. Encourage the students to add to the lists as they find other examples of alternative spellings and ask them to think about how knowing about alternative spellings will assist them when they are writing.

▼ *Publishing a class book*

When the students have listed a reasonable number of alternative spellings assist them to publish a class book. This could consist of the collated class charts or it may be a separate publication. Involve the students in deciding on the organization of the book. A contents page could be included for easy reference. Students may also like to include a page on which they each write something that they have learned about alternative spellings. The book could be placed in the class library for the students to refer to or borrow.

▼ *Students selecting words to learn*

Some of the words students select to learn may have alternative spellings, for example, *color* and *colour*. It is useful to list other words with the same alternative spelling patterns, for example, *or* — *colors, coloring, colored, uncolored, neighbor, neighborly, favor, favoring,* and so on. Ask the students to think about how this will help them with their writing.

▼ *Contacting publishers*

Publishers could be contacted to find out why they adopt a particular spelling pattern for their publications, for example, why they opt for *or* rather than *our*.

▼ *A community of writers selecting particular spelling patterns*

The class could be invited to discuss and vote on the particular spelling patterns, for example, *ize* verses *ise*, to be adopted in the classroom. The class book of alternative spellings could be shared with other classes who may then make some decisions about the spelling patterns to be adopted in their classrooms.

Games for Playing with Words

11

Anagrams

An anagram is a word or phrase that contains the same letters as another word or phrase but in a different order, for example, *ocean* and *canoe* or *Margaret Thatcher* for *that great charmer*.

Below is a list of some of the common anagrams. This list is provided as a resource of the range of anagrams and it is not intended as a list of words to be learned.

agree	eager
ideas	aside
alert	alter
beast	baste
bread	beard
bulge	bugle
burnt	brunt
cadet	acted
canoe	ocean
cents	scent
cloud	could
corps	crops
creep	crepe
dance	caned
denim	mined
early	relay

easel	lease	
elbow	below	
fibre	brief	
field	filed	
lasted	salted	
notes	onset	
marines	seminar	
nudity	untidy	
ordeal	reload	
phase	shape	
read	dare	dear
saw	was	
signed	design	singed
there	three	
volley	lovely	

Points to think about

Points to consider when students are learning about anagrams include:

▼ *Introducing anagrams*

Once students have a body of words they recognize and they are starting to think about the possible letter sequences in words, or are capable of thinking about these relationships, it is appropriate to introduce anagrams.

It is also important to consider the development of students' oral vocabulary to ensure they understand the meanings of many words that form anagrams.

▼ *Developing a sense of enjoyment in words*

One of the main reasons for teaching about anagrams is to develop in students an interest in words and a sense of enjoyment when playing with words. Anagrams were used by many writers in the past who had a fascination with language and they are often used in cryptic crosswords today.

▼ *Thinking about possible letter sequences in the English written language*

When changing the letters within an anagram to make another word it is important that the students do not have wild guesses but think about the possible letter sequences. Talk with students about how thinking about possible letter sequences will assist them when they are attempting to write unknown words in their personal writing.

▼ *Manipulating letters in anagrams — not in misspelled (jumbled) words*

The manipulation of letters in anagrams is a purposeful activity that leads students to understand the serial probability of letters in the English written language.

Changing the order of letters in anagrams allows students to manipulate letters in correctly spelled words. In contrast, jumbled word exercises, that also involve students in manipulating letters within words, present students with misspelled words — they model unconventional spellings.

A great deal of research in recent years has highlighted the power of modelling as an influential condition of learning. Consequently it is important to seriously question any activity in which an incorrect model is employed. The use of jumbled word exercises is not recommended for this reason.

▼ *Anagrams can be phrases*

Anagrams can be made from phrases, where the letters are arranged in a different order, for example, *the aristocracy* and *a rich Tory caste*.

▼ *Anagrams can have similar meanings*

Anagrams can relate to the meaning of the original word or phrase, for example, *angered* and *enraged* or *Flit on, cheering angel* for *Florence Nightingale*.

Activities

The following activities may be used to help students learn about anagrams:

▼ *Developing a class list*

As students discover anagrams in their reading and writing assist them to develop class lists for each and encourage them to add to the lists as they find other anagrams. When listing anagrams ensure the students understand their meanings and that they are words they are likely to use in their writing.

▼ *Publishing a class book*

Assist the students to publish a book of anagrams which could consist of the collated class charts or be a separate publication. The students may like to include a page on which they comment about what they have learned about anagrams and the possible letter sequences in the English written language, and how this knowledge will help them with their own writing. Place the book in the class library for the students to refer to or borrow.

▼ *Students create activities for others to complete*

To further create an interest in words students may like to write activities with anagrams for others to complete. Words used should be taken from students' writing or reading materials. For example:

1   Change the anagram. A clue may be given by underlining the first letter of the new anagram in each case:

d<u>a</u>d ....   na<u>p</u> ....

<u>h</u>ate ....   s<u>u</u>ed ....

2   Change the anagram. Anagrams could be given with verbal clues. *Dear* becomes something you accept if you are feeling courageous, that is, a ....

3   Change the anagram. Students are given an anagram that is to be changed to another anagram, then they are to make another word by adding a letter.

scale ...   laces ...   places
(anagram)   (anagram)   (new word)

Here is a clue:

Make the anagram of *scale* and get *some positions to put things.* (places)

Able was I ere I saw Elba	*aga*
anna (coin)	*Anna*
a Toyota	*dad*
deed	*deified*
ewe	*eye*
evil live	*evil olive*
Glenelg	*kayak*
Hannah	*level*
madam	*Madam, I'm Adam.*
nannan (hat)	*noon*
not on	*not a ton*
otto	*pot top*
radar	*refer*
redder	*repaper*
reviver	*rotator*
rotor	*terret (loops on harness pad)*
too hot to hoot	*Tumut*
Was it a cat I saw?	*wet stew*

Ask the students to think about how knowing about anagrams will assist them with their writing.

Resources

Augarde, Tony, *The Oxford Guide to Word Games,* Oxford University Press, 1986.

Hunter, C, *The Dictionary of Anagrams,* Routledge & Kegan Paul, London, 1982.

Palindromes

A palindrome is a word, verse or sentence that reads the same backwards as forwards.

Below is a list of common palindromes. This list is provided as a resource of the range of palindromes and it is not intended as a list of words to be learned.

Points to think about

Points to consider when students are learning about palindromes include:

▼   *Introducing palindromes*

Once students have a body of words they recognize and they are starting to think about the possible letter sequences in words, or are capable of thinking about these relationships, it is appropriate to introduce palindromes.

▼   *Developing a sense of enjoyment in words*

One of the main reasons for teaching about palindromes is to develop in students an interest in words and a sense of enjoyment when playing with words. Palindromes were used by many writers in the past who had a fascination with language.

Activities

The following activities may be used to help students learn about palindromes:

▼ *Developing a class list*

As students discover palindromes in their reading and writing assist them to develop class lists and encourage them to add to the lists as they find other palindromes.

▼ *Publishing a class book*

Assist the students to publish a book of palindromes. It could consist of the collated class charts or it may be separate publication. The students may like to include a page on which they comment about what they have learned about palindromes and the possible letter sequences in the English written language and how this knowledge will help them with their own writing. Place the book in the class library for the students to refer to or borrow.

Resources

Augarde, Tony, *The Oxford Guide to Word Games,* Oxford University Press, 1986.

General games

It may become apparent during discussions with students or from reading their writing that further clarification of their understandings about various aspects of the English written language is necessary. If this is so, students could play games like those following and could create similar activities for their peers to complete. The words selected for the games should be taken from class lists, students' writing and reading materials, lists of words they have selected to learn, topic lists, and other sources that are relevant to them.

Some games may be adapted and played with more than one type of word and with words that have different features, for example, *Memory* may be played with contractions, compound words, shortened words, words with a common spelling pattern, and so on. The types of words or words with particular features that could be used with each game are indicated under the heading *Types of words/word features.*

After a game has been played, for example, *Noughts and Crosses* with homophones, talk with the students about what they have learned, in this instance about homophones, and how this will assist them with their writing.

Note: Where the term *suffix* is used it indicates suffixes other than those that form plurals, comparatives and superlatives.

Word Sorts

Types of words/word features: A mixture of different types of words and words with many different features — homophones, plurals, compound words, prefixes, suffixes, derivatives, common spelling pattern, common sound, comparatives and superlatives, word families, contractions, acronyms, eponyms, anagrams, shortened words, blended words and alternate spellings.

Players: 2-4 per group

Materials: Approximately 20 pieces of light cardboard for each player

Method:

1 Players, as a group, select approximately 20 words from class lists, personal spelling lists, their reading and personal writing.

2 Each player makes a copy of the 20 words — each word is written on a separate piece of paper.

3 Players, all at the same time, sort their group of 20 words according to their own criteria. This could vary from player to player. Criteria used could be contractions, a particular spelling pattern or suffix, and so on. A record may be kept of the number of groups and the criteria used for sorting the words, for example, the suffix *ing*.

4 The player who creates the greatest number of groups is a winner and the player who creates the greatest number in a group is also a winner. Thus there may be two winners.

5 The words are kept and added to a wordbank. The word sort is then repeated, using another group of 20 words. The first lot of 20 words may be added to this lot for sorting, and this step repeated so that the number of words available for sorting steadily increases.

    Note: A word sort may be made more difficult by sorting words which contain one common feature only, such as the suffix *ing*. The students can then sort the words according to whether the final consonant has been doubled, where the *y* has been changed to *i* before adding *ing,* or where the final *e* has been deleted before adding *ing*.

Noughts and Crosses

Types of words/word features: Homophones, word family, anagrams
Players: 2 groups of 4 players, a captain to direct the game (9 altogether)
Materials: Paper, stopwatch, wordbooks and dictionaries
Method:
1 Players organize team members, choose a player to represent each team and select a 'captain' to run the game.
2 The squares for the traditional game of noughts and crosses are drawn.
3 Each team lists six words with a common feature, such as homophones, and writes a sentence that contains each homophone and indicates its meaning. For example, if the homophone is *meat* the sentence could be '*Meat* is the flesh of animals'. The team also lists other homophones from the set on the same piece of paper.

Team 1
Sentence *1. meat Meat is the flesh of animals.*

Homophone from same set *meet*

Team 2
Sentence *2. their Their team is winning the match.*

Homophone from same set *there*

Homophone from same set *they're*

4 Players decide on the time allowed for the team representatives to give

4 Players decide on the time allowed for the team representatives to give an answer.
5 Each team gives their list of six homophones and sentences to the captain. The captain uses those written by Team 1 for the Team 2 representative to answer. The captain calls out the first homophone, then the sentence that contains the homophone.
6 The representative from Team 2 writes down another homophone from the set and gives a sentence that contains and indicates the meaning of that homophone. In the example above the homophone for *meat* is *meet*. If the captain decides that the homophone is spelt correctly and the sentence is correct and given within the time limit, the player puts a cross on the grid.
7 The representative from Team 1 is then read the first homophone and sentence written by Team 2, and if the player answers correctly and in time that player places a nought on the grid.
8 The representative from Team 1 is then read the second homophone and sentence written by Team 2, and so on. Team members are able to assist their representatives by referring to dictionaries and wordbooks. The game continues until there is a winner.

Memory

Types of words/word features: Homophones, plurals, compound words, common spelling pattern, common sound, word family, contractions, acronyms, anagrams, shortened words, blended words, prefixes and suffixes.
Players: 2
Materials: Approximately 20 small pieces of cardboard
Method:
1 Players select approximately 20 words with a common feature, for example, plurals, from class lists, personal spelling lists, their reading and personal writing, dictionaries and wordbooks. They prepare cards for the game *Memory* by writing the singular and plural forms of the listed words on cards. They write one word on each card, for example, *pouch* on one card and *pouches* on another.
2 Cards are shuffled and placed face down on the table.
3 Each player takes a turn to place two cards face-up. When two cards that match are turned up, that is, the singular and plural form of word, the player picks these up and has another turn.

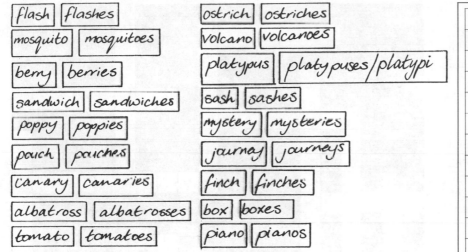

flash | flashes
mosquito | mosquitoes
berry | berries
sandwich | sandwiches
poppy | poppies
pouch | pouches
canary | canaries
albatross | albatrosses
tomato | tomatoes

ostrich | ostriches
volcano | volcanoes
platypus | platypuses/platypi
sash | sashes
mystery | mysteries
journey | journeys
finch | finches
box | boxes
piano | pianos

4 The winner is the player with the most cards at the end of the game.

Word mazes

Types of words/word features: Any type of word with a common feature is appropriate.
Player: 1
Materials: *Super Wordfind,* dictionary or wordbook
Method:

Decide what the focus of the maze is to be, for example, the prefix *un*. Use the computing software *Super Wordfind* (see Resources, page 149) to create a maze. Players find as many words as they can, using a dictionary or wordbook to help them. Ensure that all words written in the maze are spelled from left to right and from top to bottom. The significance of modelling conventional spelling cannot be overstated.

    Note: This activity may be varied by listing the words to be found in the maze. Students could then refer to these words for assistance. Talk with the students about how such an activity can assist them with their writing.

A	B	U	N	A	T	T	R	A	C	T	I	V	E	C	F	I	U	D
Q	U	N	P	L	E	A	S	A	U	T	J	H	U	G	U	E	N	U
O	U	N	P	L	E	A	S	A	N	T	K	U	N	K	N	O	W	N
N	P	E	R	W	X	S	V	M	H	L	T	N	R	F	E	I	I	D
U	N	C	O	M	F	O	R	T	A	B	L	E	E	H	X	E	L	R
N	A	E	U	N	K	I	N	D	P	S	R	V	A	Z	P	G	L	E
D	Z	S	Y	U	N	T	I	U	P	U	Q	E	L	A	E	P	I	S
O	P	S	U	N	L	U	C	K	Y	P	U	N	L	O	C	K	N	S
N	C	A	E	B	J	C	E	J	V	U	N	O	Q	O	T	B	G	J
E	F	R	B	G	A	W	I	F	U	N	G	R	A	T	E	F	U	L
G	U	Y	Y	X	K	H	D	K	L	H	M	W	R	N	D	C	N	U
U	N	N	U	M	B	E	R	E	D	E	V	U	N	D	O	M	C	N
U	C	S	L	H	I	U	C	T	Z	A	Y	V	X	S	Y	D	O	L
M	O	K	L	Z	U	N	E	M	P	L	O	Y	E	D	W	T	N	I
R	V	Q	P	M	H	F	I	Y	S	T	Q	R	V	K	L	E	S	K
D	E	U	N	L	O	A	D	U	A	H	U	N	T	I	D	Y	C	E
E	R	N	G	N	O	I	C	K	B	Y	P	X	W	Z	J	F	I	L
M		F	O	T	L	R	J	U	N	N	A	T	U	R	A	L	O	Y
U	N	R	E	L	I	A	B	L	E	U	N	A	B	L	E	G	U	I
U	N	B	E	L	I	E	V	A	B	L	E	D	A	U	H	B	S	X

WORDS TO LOOK FOR:

uncomfortable	unhappy	unbelievable	unconscious
unhealthy	uncover	undress	unknown
unnumbered	undo	unkind	unnatural
unemployed	unlucky	unreliable	unexpected
unlock	undone	uneven	unload
unable	unfair	unnecessary	unwilling
ungrateful	unpleasant	unreal	untidy

*A word maze that focuses on the prefix **un**. All the words are written in the correct direction and words are listed to provide students with an additional visual image to refer to.*

Crosswords

Types of words/word features: Homophones, plurals, compound words, prefixes, suffixes, derivatives, comparatives and superlatives, common spelling pattern, common sound, word family, acronyms, eponyms, anagrams, shortened words, blended words and so on.

Player: 1

Materials: *Crossword Magic*

Method:

1 Decide what the focus of the crossword is to be, for example, compound words formed from some of the 100 Common Words. Use the computing software *Crossword Magic* (see Resources, page 149) to create a crossword.

2 Enter words (answers) and clues for the crossword. Where possible the clues for the crossword should be spelling clues, not meaning-related clues. For example:

Answer	Clue
everyone	every + one
someone	some + one
nothing	no + thing
nobody	no + body

Across

2 no + where =
5 any + thing =
6 some + body =
8 every + where =
9 any + one =
12 no + thing =
13 some + thing =
14 any + where =

Down

1 every + body =
3 every +one =
4 some + where =
6 some + one =
7 every + thing =
10 no + body =
11 any + body =

A crossword based on high frequency words. Clues are spelling clues and assist students to understand the meaning relationships between compound words and the smaller words that form them.

Snap

Types of words/word features: Homophones, plurals, compound words, prefixes, suffixes, derivatives, common spelling pattern, common sound, comparatives and superlatives, word family, contractions, acronyms, eponyms, anagrams, shortened words and blended words.

Players: 2

Materials: 20 small pieces of cardboard

Method:

1 Players list ten words with a common feature, such as contractions and the two words from which they were formed, for example:

Contraction	Two words that form contraction
they'd	they had *or* they would
they've	they have
they're	they are
we'd	we had *or* we would
we'll	we will
we're	we are
I'd	I had *or* I would
I'm	I am
he's	he is *or* he has
she's	she is *or* she has

2 Each contraction is written on a card, for example *they'd* on one card and the two words from which it was formed, for example, *they had* on another card.

3 The cards are separated into two packs — one for contractions, the other for the words from which they were formed.

4 Each player takes a pack of cards and then takes a turn to place a card face-up on a pile in the middle. When two cards that match (a contraction and the words from which it was formed) are placed on top of one another the first player to say *Snap* wins the pile of cards.

5 The winner is the player with the most cards at the end of the game.

Bingo

Types of words/word features: Homophones, plurals, compound words, prefixes, suffixes, derivatives, common spelling pattern, common sound, comparatives and superlatives, word family, contractions, acronyms, eponyms, anagrams, shortened words and blended words.

Players: Any number

Materials: A piece of paper with 12 squares for each player
A list of 12 words for each player
12 buttons or other markers for each player

Method:

1 Players (as a group) select and list 24 words with a common feature, such as belonging to the same word family. Two words are selected from twelve word families, for example:

come	coming	have	having
down	sundown	was	wasn't
has	hasn't	house	houses
start	started	where	wherever
home	homeless	get	getting
with	without	after	afternoon

2 One word from each word family is listed, for example, *come*, *have* and *down*, and so on. Each player is then given a list of the 12 selected words.

3 Players are given a piece of paper with 12 squares.

4 They write a word from the list in each of the 12 squares. It is their choice where they put the words.

5 The remaining 12 words from the word families are read out and kept in the order in which they are read. As the words are called out the players put markers on the matching word from the word family. For example, if *have* is read out, players mark *having*. The first player who has a row or diagonal filled calls out *Bingo* and reads the words aloud.

Scrabble

Types of words/word features: Any type of word with a common feature is appropriate.

Players: 2-4

Materials: A board marked in squares
Many small square cards with letters of the alphabet

Method:

1　Players decide on the focus of game, for example, the prefix *re*.

2　Players make many small square cards — each with a letter of the alphabet on it plus a score. To ensure there are sufficient letters to make the words containing the prefix *re* the *re* words are listed and several copies made of the letters from each word. The letters should be written in upper case.

3　The cards are placed on the table face down.

4　Each player takes seven cards.

5　Each player has a turn at making a word with the prefix *re* using their letters. Players may use a dictionary or wordbook to help them. Each card used to form a word is replaced. For example, if two letters are used in a word a player selects another two cards.

6　The game continues until all the cards have been used or it is impossible to make a *re* word. The winner is the player with the highest score.

　　Note: The students may like to make up some rules of their own about doubling scores, adding letters to existing words, and so on. These rules could be written on a chart and referred to.

Card Carpet

Types of words/word features: Common spelling pattern, common sound

Players: 2

Materials: 20 small pieces of cardboard
A board marked in 15 squares (the same size as the small pieces of card)
Die, stop watch

Method:

1　Each player lists ten words with a common feature, such as a common sound — the /**k**/ sound — this makes a total of 20 /**k**/ words. Players should check to ensure a variety of spelling patterns that represent the /**k**/ sound is included.

2　Players write the words on separate cards.

3　Players place the words on the board — one per square, making sure that the words in each row represent a variety of spelling patterns, for example, bro**cc**oli, **c**aravan, yo**lk**, zu**cch**ini, wi**ck**et, **wh**iskers, and so on.

4　Players choose a spelling pattern that represents the /**k**/ sound. For example Player 1 may choose the spelling pattern *ch* and may only move along a path of words where the spelling pattern *ch* represents the /**k**/ sound. Player 2 may choose the spelling pattern *ck* and may only move along a path of words where *ck* represents the /**k**/ sound.

stick	cake	whiskers	zucchini
clinic	stomach	broccoli	yolk
monarch	wicket	cactus	kick
caravan	brick	Christmas	baking
work	crack	school	cricket

A card carpet based on the /k/ sound which is represented by many different letters and spelling patterns.

5 Players throw a dice and move accordingly. They take turns to find a path across the 'card carpet'. They can move in any direction but must be able to land on a word that contains the spelling pattern they have chosen.
6 Players identify each word they land on and then pick up the card. The player who picks up the most words within a given time is the winner.
7 Players can play the game again by using other /k/ words or by rearranging those they have.

Resources

Crossword Magic, L & S Computerware, Mindscape.
Super Wordfind, Hartley Courseware, Dataflow.

Resources

Bolton, Faye, & Snowball, Diane, *Ideas for Spelling,* Heinemann, Portsmouth, NH, 1993.

Bryson, Bill, *The Penguin Dictionary of Troublesome Words,* Penguin, Harmondsworth, 1984.

Carroll, David, *The Dictionary of Foreign Terms in the English Language,* Hawthorn Books, New York, 1973.

Hall, Timothy, *How Things Start,* Collins, Sydney, 1979.

Jones, David (comp.), *The Australian Dictionary of Acronyms and Abbreviations,* Second Back Row Press, Leura, NSW, 1981.

Morris, William, & Morris, Mary, *Dictionary of Word and Phrase Origins,* Harper & Rowe, New York, 1962.

Partridge, Eric, *Usage and Abusage,* Penguin, Harmondsworth, 1973.

Pickles, Colin, & Meynell, Laurence, *The Beginning of Words — How English Grew,* Anthony Blond, London, 1970.

Pugh, E. A. *A Dictionary of Acronyms and Abbreviations,* Clive Bingley, London, 1970.

Roget's Thesaurus of Words and Phrases (many publishers).

Shipley, Joseph T., *Dictionary of Word Origins,* Littlefield, Adams & Co. Iowa, 1957.